# BIG TOP BURNING

## The True Story of an Arsonist, a Missing Girl, and The Greatest Show On Earth

### LAURA A. WOOLLETT

CHICAGO
REVIEW
PRESS

Published by Chicago Review Press Incorporated
814 North Franklin Street
Chicago, Illinois 60610

ISBN 978-1-61373-114-7

Library of Congress Cataloging-in-Publication Data

Woollett, Laura A.
  Big top burning : the story of an arsonist, a missing girl, and
the greatest show on earth / Laura A. Woollett.
     pages cm
  Includes bibliographical references and index.
  ISBN 978-1-61373-114-7 (cloth)
  1. Hartford Circus Fire, Hartford, Conn., 1944—Juvenile literature. 2. Fires--Connecticut—Hartford—History—Juvenile literature. 3. Arson--Connecticut—Hartford—History—Juvenile
literature. 4. Ringling Brothers Barnum and Bailey Combined
Shows--History--Juvenile literature. 5. Dead—Identification—
Case studies—Juvenile literature. 6. Hartford (Conn.)—History—20th century—Juvenile literature.  I. Title.

  F104.H3W66 2015
  974.6'3042—dc23

                                    2014036121
Interior design: Sarah Olson
Map illustration: James Spence

Photograph of Emmett Kelly on page [43] by Ralph Emerson Sr.
Every effort has been made to contact the copyright holder. The
editors would welcome information concerning any inadvertent
errors or omissions.

Printed in the United States of America
5  4  3  2  1

## FOR DAD

*Those remembered are never lost.*

# CONTENTS

*Prologue* • 1

ONE: The Circus Comes to Town • 3

TWO: "The Greatest Show On Earth" • 13

THREE: Fire! • 23

FOUR: "The Day the Clowns Cried" • 37

FIVE: Municipal Hospital • 55

SIX: "Who Knows This Child?" • 65

SEVEN: Who Was to Blame? • 81

EIGHT: Accident or Arson? • 93

NINE: A Name for Little Miss 1565 • 115

*Author's Note* • 133

*Acknowledgments* • 137

*Notes* • 139

*Bibliography* • 147

*Image Credits* • 157

*Index* • 161

# PROLOGUE

Some say they saw the flickering of a small flame on the side wall of the tent just above the men's bathroom. At first no one moved; surely the circus staff had it under control. But by the time circus workers reached the fire, their meager buckets of water had little effect. As the crowd watched, the flame grew, spidering up the tent wall. Then someone yelled, "Fire!" and the panic began. A frightened crowd of 6,000 spectators began jostling down the rickety bleachers and across the grandstand toward the exits. The mob shoved aside folding chairs and anything else in the way. People tripped and fell. Some women and children were plucked up off the ground by kind, strong hands.

Others were trampled under the rush of frantic feet. A crush of bodies pushed toward the main entrance on the west end of the tent. The northeast and northwest exits were blocked by tall steel chutes where snarling panthers still prowled inside.

Meanwhile, the blaze spread across the ceiling of the massive big top, fueled by the mixture of wax and gasoline that was used to waterproof the tent. Pieces of flaming canvas floated to the ground and black smoke billowed, making it difficult to breathe. As the fire grew, the tent became an oven. Parents desperately struggled to hold on to their small children as everyone was swept along in the swarm of people rushing toward the exits.

The tent burned to the ground in fewer than 10 minutes, and 167 people died. It was one of the worst tragedies the country had ever seen. From the ashes, questions arose: How did the fire start? Was it an accident? Could a madman have set it on purpose? Who cared for the people who survived? Who were the victims? How did investigators identify them from their charred remains?

The mysteries surrounding the Hartford circus fire are still being explored today, more than 70 years after the disaster occurred. Professionals and amateurs alike have examined the evidence and argued their theories. Now it's your turn.

# 1

# THE CIRCUS COMES TO TOWN

*"Coming from Providence on its own trains of red and yellow steel cars, Ringling Brothers and Barnum and Bailey Circus arrives in Hartford this morning."*

—Hartford Courant, *July 5, 1944*

You could almost hear the buzz of excitement in the air over Hartford, Connecticut, leading up to the arrival of the one and only Ringling Bros. and Barnum & Bailey Circus. Posters plastered on buildings and storefronts boasted the show's highlights: Mr. and Mrs. Gargantua the Great, a pair of enormous gorillas; aerialists performing a Cloud Ballet; and a pantomime by the famous clown Emmett Kelly.

Emmett Kelly was a "tramp clown." He dressed in drab colors and painted a large white frown and black stubble on his face. His routine was different from those of other, more colorful clowns, whose slapstick antics were intended to make people laugh. Instead, without speaking a word, Kelly made people feel sorry for him. Poor Weary Willie, the audience thought, chuckling as he tried unsuccessfully to sweep a circle of light into a dustpan. By the summer of 1944, Kelly had been traveling with the Ringling Bros. circus for three years, and Weary Willie was one of its most popular attractions.

In the 1940s, a trip to the circus was a rare treat. Though Hartford was a thriving city during the years of World War II, the average income was only about $52 a week. Many fathers and husbands served in the military overseas. More women entered the work force when they found themselves raising their families on their own. Kids often contributed to the family income or made their own pocket money by delivering groceries or newspapers. Buying food and paying rent took priority, and circus tickets were expensive—the nicer grandstand seats cost $1.20 each. But for an occasion as big as the Ringling Bros. circus, families saved their pennies all year long.

A poem in the circus program promised "the real Fairyland is right at hand, it's where the circus holds sway." Going to the circus was not only a delight for children; it gave everyone a break from the real world. Emmett Kelly claimed people loved the circus because "they want to laugh and forget their troubles." Worries about food rationing or bomb shelters faded away amid the bright colors and lively music of "The Greatest Show On Earth."

Even the government thought the circus was good for the morale of the country. During the war, railroad travel was restricted so that military supplies and machinery could be transported quickly and efficiently. However, the Ringling Bros. circus was given special permission to use the rails to travel from town to town. The government also used the circus to promote the sale of war bonds. People who bought bonds were loaning their money to the government to pay for the war. After the war was over, people could cash in the bonds and get their money back, plus interest. In addition, anyone who bought war bonds was given free circus tickets.

With many men fighting overseas, there was a shortage of staff to run the circus. Ringling Bros. placed this advertisement in *Billboard* magazine: "Good Salary and Expenses Offered to Ambitious Young Men Who are

Not Subject to Call in the Armed Forces. Learn the Art of Outdoor Advertising with the Greatest Show On Earth." They also hired local boys in the towns where they stopped. Too young to enlist in the military, the boys had free time and were eager to help out. They took care of the animals by filling their troughs with water from fire hydrants, and they spread straw and sawdust on the ground. The older, stronger boys served as roustabouts. Roustabouts helped set up and take down the tents and did other physical labor around the grounds. Young boys made 50¢ for a day's work or received free passes to the show. Many kids thought that being part of the action and getting a free ticket to see the amazing Ringling Bros. circus was even better than money.

At the end of June 1944, 15-year-old Robert Segee thought he'd like to get a closer look at The Greatest Show On Earth. Robert lived with his parents and siblings in Portland, Maine. He was a tall boy, and strong, much bigger than other kids his age. Robert had few friends, though, and he hadn't done well in school. Because he had been kept back several times, he was older than all his classmates. Brooding and quiet, Robert spent most of his time alone in his room. To make matters worse, Robert and his father did not get along. Mr. Segee bullied Robert and yelled at him often.

He always seemed to be punishing Robert for small mistakes.

So Robert ran away from home and joined the Ringling Bros. circus when it came to Portland. The manager of the lighting department, Edward "Whitey" Versteeg, gave Robert a job setting up the wiring and lights in the big top. Later, Robert proudly told people he had even worked the main spotlight during the shows.

Everyone in the circus family had been looking forward to the summer season. The performers and workers got settled in the train cars in which they lived and traveled. Animal trainers practiced their acts with the elephants and the panthers. The season had been off to a good start until the show reached Portland. There, the crew discovered a small fire on the tent ropes. Luckily, it was put out immediately and caused no real damage. The show went on without incident.

At the next stop in Providence, Rhode Island, bad luck struck again when a small blaze appeared on a tent flap. Like the flame in Portland, it was quickly extinguished before it did any harm. There was always dry straw on the ground for the animals, and cigarette smoking was common. So the staff wasn't alarmed when small fires popped up once in a while. The seat hands (circus workers who manned the bleachers and grandstand) were always able to put them out quickly with buckets of water placed throughout the tent. A cause for the fires in Portland and Providence was never determined, and the traveling show continued on its way.

As the circus was rolling into Hartford, the Cook family was enjoying a reunion. Nine-year-old Donald, eight-year-old Eleanor, and six-year-old Edward were visiting their mother, Mildred. Life had not been easy for the Cooks. Mildred's husband had recently abandoned his family, and Mildred suddenly needed a way to support her children. She got a job at an insurance company in Hartford and left Donald, Eleanor, and Edward in the care of her brother and sister-in-law, Ted and Marion Parsons, in Southampton, Massachusetts. While Uncle Ted and Aunt Marion were like a second set of parents to the children, they were excited about this special visit with their mother. They had taken the train from Southampton and couldn't wait to see the wild animal acts and silly red-nosed clowns.

The Ringling Bros. three-ring circus was scheduled to perform four shows in Hartford: two on July 5, and two on July 6. Mildred had tickets for the matinee on July 5, but when she and the children arrived at the circus grounds, they saw that the tents were not yet up. There was no smell of fresh, buttery popcorn in the air. There were no sideshow barkers enticing people to gawk at human oddities. The grounds were a mess of canvas tenting, ropes, and half-assembled food stalls.

Confusion on the tracks had held up the circus train for several hours on its way from Providence to Hartford. The performers and crew finally reached the grounds at 350 Barbour Street around noon, but it was too late. There was not enough time to get the big top and the side tents ready for the matinee. Disappointed circus-goers clutched their tickets, wondering what to

Donald, Eleanor, and Edward Cook.

do. The staff told everyone to return for the matinee the following afternoon. Mildred exchanged her tickets and assured her children that they would not miss out on the show.

The Ringling Bros. crew was disheartened at the train's late arrival. But there was still work to do, including setting up the enormous big top. The main tent was massive. It was 450 feet long and 200 feet wide—one-third longer than an entire football field.

The Ringling Bros. circus big top tent, circa 1944.

Elephants pulled on the ropes, hoisting 75,000 square feet of heavy canvas into position. Trainers got the animals comfortable, and the cook prepared food for the tired, hungry crew.

After the grounds were ready, Robert Segee ate with the rest of the crew and the performers in the mess tent, waiting for the evening show to begin. Many performers were superstitious about missing a show and considered their late arrival a bad omen.

# 2

# "THE GREATEST SHOW ON EARTH"

---

*"The last word in high wire thrillers, new hazardous and hair raising feats by world acclaimed artists who shake dice with death at dizzy heights."*

—*description of the Flying Wallendas in the 1944
Ringling Bros. and Barnum & Bailey Circus program*

---

**M**ore than 6,000 people attended the circus on that hot July 6 afternoon. Circus programs became fans, and men pulled handkerchiefs from back pockets to wipe their sweaty brows. "The air was stagnant. There was no breeze," Arthur S. Lassow recalled. With high humidity and temperatures in the 80s, the muggy air seemed to cling to the skin. It's no wonder the stand selling glass bottles of Coca-Cola was a big hit. A long chug of ice-cold soda pop hit the spot.

Before entering the big top, people could wander through the animal menagerie—a traveling zoo where you could see the animals up close. The Ringling Bros. circus was home to many unusual and amazing creatures including: 1 anoa buffalo, 1 cassowary, 1 hartebeest, 1 pygmy hippopotamus and 2 large common hippos, 1 kangaroo, 1 llama, 1 mandrill, 1 springbok, 1 white-bearded gnu, 2 bears, 2 cranes, 2 donkeys, 2 giraffes, 2 gorillas, 2 guanacos, 2 king vultures, 2 lions, 2 tigers, 2 zebras, 3 chimpanzees, 3 cockatoos, 5 camels, 19 rhesus monkeys, 30 elephants, and 117 horses!

Betty Lou, the pygmy hippo, was a crowd favorite. She kept cool by wading in the water of her tank as patrons smiled over her. Betty Lou was one of the animals that had survived a fire in 1942, when a spark from a passing train had ignited the menagerie tent. The flames had spread quickly, and the staff could do little to stop it. All hands did their best to lead the animals to safety. No circus workers or audience members were hurt, but 45 animals died. Now, two years later, many of the animals in the menagerie were survivors of that tragedy. Old wounds had healed, and new animals had joined the show. People once again marveled at the long necks of the giraffes and the big humps of the camels. The disaster of 1942 seemed a distant memory.

Besides the animal menagerie, the circus offered sideshows before the main event. Sideshows presented a curious assortment that included sword swallowers, bearded ladies, and tattooed men. In one sideshow attraction, Gargantua the giant gorilla and his "wife,"

Children visit the elephants in the menagerie.

another large gorilla, sat quietly in their cage as people ogled them through the bars. Today, sideshows are considered cruel and inappropriate, but in the 1940s they were common. Among the acts that thrilled audiences in 1944 were Rasmus Neilsen, the tattooed strong man; Miss Patricia, swallower of neon tubes; Señorita Carmen, snake trainer; the Doll Family (Harry, Gracie, Daisey, and Tiny), the "world's smallest people"; Percy Pape, the living skeleton; Louis Long, the sword swallower; Egan Twist, the rubber-armed man; Kutty Singlee, the fireproof man; and Mr. and Mrs. Fischer, a giant and giantess.

All around the grounds were stalls where vendors sold programs and other souvenirs. One vendor even sold chameleons on little string leashes. When eight-year-old Donald Gale's mother bought him one, he carefully tucked the lizard into his shirt pocket to keep it safe.

Families enjoyed hot dogs and ice cream. Children's faces were sticky with cotton candy, and the intoxicating smell of freshly roasted peanuts lingered in the air. Residents of the nearby neighborhood set up lemonade stands and sold cool drinks.

Nine-year-old Eugene Badger got to go to the circus as a birthday treat. Eugene and his father headed to the circus grounds while Mrs. Badger went to the

Children enjoy a treat before the show.

Red Cross to donate blood. Eugene and his father did
not spend much time outside the tent before the show.
They couldn't afford things like candy apples and sideshows, which cost extra. Instead, they made their way

through the main entrance on the west end of the tent. Mr. Badger had a medical condition and used crutches to get around, so Eugene helped his father as they walked the length of the tent to their seats in the northeast bleachers.

Bleacher seats took up the four corners of the tent. The grandstand seats ran along the sides, where folding chairs were set up on wooden boards. These seats had backs, making them more comfortable and therefore more expensive. Unlike today's big arenas where seats are bolted to the floor, the grandstand chairs were free standing. People had to be careful not to knock over the chairs as they walked across the wooden planks.

The Cook family sat in the southwest grandstand. Like everyone else in the tent that day, Mildred and her children were eager to laugh at the clowns and to gasp in wonder at the acrobats and animal tamers. It was hot inside the tent, but at least the canvas roof gave protection from the blazing sun.

As the band warmed up the clowns put on their makeup and the Flying Wallendas, the famous trapeze artists, got ready to take the stage. Seat hands stationed themselves beneath the bleachers. During the show they would pick up trash and watch to make sure no one snuck in without paying. They also had the very important job of guarding against accidents, including

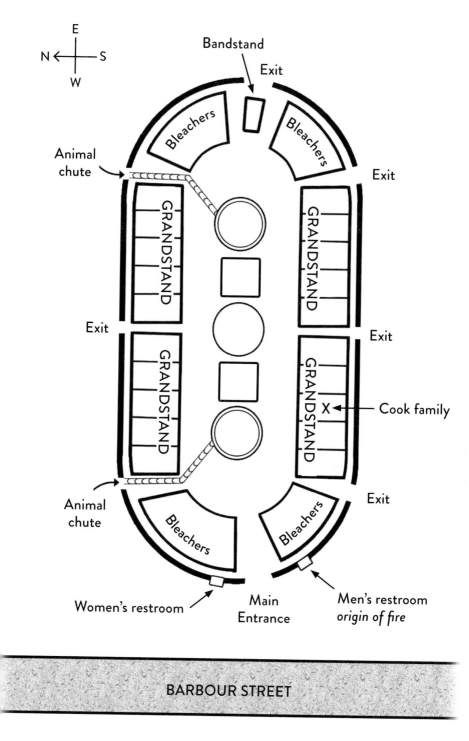

Map showing the interior of the big top tent.

fires. Smoking was not allowed in the big top, but this rule was difficult to enforce. In the 1940s, smoking was more common than it is today. Buckets of water were placed beneath each seating section before the show. If a seat hand saw a carelessly tossed cigarette or burning match fall from the stands, he could quickly put it out.

At 2:23 PM, the show began. Up first was a comedy act in which girls in bright sequined costumes "tamed" a performer dressed in a lion suit. Next came May Kovar and Joseph Walsh and their performances with real wild cats on opposite ends of the tent. Known as the "lion queen" of the circus, May astounded audiences with her bravery and control of the large, snarling felines. In Hartford, May deftly led 15 leopards, panthers, and pumas through their tricks as the audience watched, spellbound. Meanwhile, Joseph performed with lions, polar bears, and Great Danes.

"I was awestruck at the enormity of how large the [big cats] really were, never having seen a wild animal like that," circus-goer Anthony Pastizzo recalled. "And to see them performing with a human inside that cage, I was really amazed at how anyone gathered enough courage to work with an animal that size and as ferocious as that [cat]!"

May performed with masterful artistry when most people would be shaking with fear. In fact, just the year before, May had been attacked by one of her cats during a performance. A jaguar had leapt off of its perch toward her, teeth bared. May fended him off, but the jaguar attacked a second time, digging its dagger-sharp claws into her chest. Her injuries had required dozens of stitches. Performers like May enjoyed their work, but it could be a dangerous job.

At the end of their act, May and Joseph left the floor, and the Flying Wallendas began to take their places on a platform 30 feet in the air. The Wallendas—Karl, Helen, Joe, Herman, and Henrietta—were world famous for their performances. Karl and Helen's daughter Carla, only four at the time, would eventually join them. The troupe's high-wire pyramid was especially astounding. Joe and Herman pedaled bicycles on the high wire while holding a wooden board between them. On this board, Karl balanced himself precariously on a chair. Helen miraculously completed the pyramid, standing atop her husband's shoulders.

As the Wallendas climbed rope ladders to their platforms, the busy circus staff kept the show moving on the ground. May and Joseph guided their animals into long steel and wooden corridors called chutes, which led to cages outside the big top. Because the chutes blocked both the northeast and northwest exits, they needed to be removed after the animals had passed through. Moving the chutes was a difficult task, and because the circus was short on staff, some of the seat hands had to leave their stations to help.

At about 2:40 PM, no seat hands were left to monitor the area by the southwest bleachers. It was then that someone first noticed a small flame flickering on the side wall of the tent.

# 3

# FIRE!

*"We heard a roar, like the applause when one of the big acts comes off, only we knew that the animal act was over and there shouldn't be applause. . . . Then we smelled smoke."*
—Providence Journal, *July 7, 1944*

Donalda LaVoie, age 15, grew worried when she saw the grapefruit-sized flame. "There's a fire over there!" she told her uncle and pointed across the tent to an area just above the men's restroom. "Don't worry about it. Someone will put it out," her uncle assured her. But no one did.

High above the crowd, the Wallendas also noticed the flame, which had quickly grown in size. Karl Wallenda knew it could be dangerous. He told his family to get down from the high wire as fast as they could.

More and more people began to notice the fire, which was spreading rapidly up the side wall. Finally some seat hands ran over to douse the flames, but their buckets of water were not enough to fight the blaze. Tragically, no fire extinguishers had been placed inside the tent. Instead, they were still packed inside a truck hundreds of yards away.

Barbara Wallis Felgate, who was just six years old at the time, was too busy staring at the big cats to notice the fire at first. "I was watching the lions . . . go out," she said. Then she saw a flickering light. "I remember the music changing." The band struck up the first loud, staccato notes of "Stars and Stripes Forever," a signal to the circus hands that there was danger in the tent. Termed the "Disaster March," this tune had long been used to alert the performers and staff when there was a problem, as well as to soothe the audience and prevent a panic.

Hearing the music, the circus hands were quick to get moving. The audience, however, did not know how to react. For a moment, some people wondered if it was all part of the show. But when someone shouted, "Fire!" it became clear this was a true emergency.

Subdued confusion suddenly turned to frenzy. As the blaze grew, the spectators knew they had to get out of the tent, and get out fast. An announcer's voice came over the loudspeaker, telling everyone to remain calm. Some people kept their composure and moved quickly and quietly out the nearest exit. Twelve-year-old Rose Norrie, her younger sister Antoinette, and their brother Frank were able to make it out the main entrance before it got too crowded. "I came right through the doorway," Rose said.

Unfortunately, many others were not so composed. Terribly frightened, some people pushed over chairs and shoved their way through the crowd to get out. Others even knocked people down to save themselves.

"I grabbed the hand of my niece Judy and proceeded to walk out to the aisle," Margaret D'Abatto recalled in her witness statement to police. "But within a second's time the aisle had been completely covered with chairs. . . . We began climbing over chairs, and at one time, someone had pushed my niece down under one of the collapsible chairs. I helped her up immediately and kept her in front of me so that she would not be knocked down again."

Mildred Cook and her three children were several rows up in the southwest grandstand when people started rushing out. Donald wanted to take his brother and sister with him, but Mildred pulled the younger children back to her. "You go along," Mildred told her oldest child. It was then that the Cooks separated.

The big top on fire.

Mildred, holding Edward's and Eleanor's hands, made her way down to the massive crowd fighting to get out the main entrance. Donald instead climbed to the top of the grandstand and jumped nimbly down the back. Lifting up the side wall of the tent, where it was loose from the ground, he crawled underneath the canvas to safety.

Others also found alternate ways to escape. Thirteen-year-old Donald Anderson helped hundreds of people, including his older cousin, escape by using his pocket-knife to cut the ropes fastened to a stake that held the tent tight to the ground. He was then able to lift the canvas wall and escape by crawling underneath. "[I] noticed a girl about five years old lying on the ground—her arm seemed injured. I picked her up and got her out safely," Donald wrote in a letter to the governor of Connecticut. Donald's story was widely reported in the newspapers. Though it always made him uncomfortable, Donald was seen as a hero, and people from all over sent letters congratulating him for his quick thinking.

The Wallendas were still up on the wire when Eugene Badger and his father noticed the fire. "When the fire broke out, everyone got up to run. But my father told me to sit, and I'm watching [the tent] burn." Once everyone had left their area of the bleachers, Mr. Badger used a seat to break through the boards below

View from the field just beyond the burning circus tent.

them. Then he dropped his son through the hole and jumped down to the ground after him. Eugene helped his father back up onto his crutches, and together they looked for an exit. "Twice before we got out my father was knocked down by two males. One of them stopped to help him up, but the other one didn't." Eugene and his father finally escaped through a hole cut in the tent's wall. "I remember looking back underneath [the bleachers], seeing the burning tent falling on people." Mr. Badger's calm reaction to the chaos had saved his son and himself. They escaped unhurt.

Lorena Dutelle and her mother attended the circus together that day. Because her father had died some years earlier, Lorena and her mother were very close. Mrs. Dutelle always wore a gold locket containing a picture of her husband, young and smart looking in his round black glasses. The two felt he had been watching over them that frightful day. They were among the lucky ones who got out safely.

Soon the air inside the tent grew thick with smoke, and the fire had spread all the way up the side wall and onto the roof. Pieces of flaming canvas dropped down upon the crowd. The wax that had been used to waterproof the tent melted and dripped onto the people below, causing horrible burns.

Seven-year-old Elliot Smith got caught in the swarm of people pushing toward the main entrance. "My hand got torn out of my mother's. So there I was, alone, getting shoved and carried along with the crowd. Actually, I started punching with my fists, trying to make room for myself. . . . Until finally, I got knocked down."

Meanwhile, Mildred Cook tried to hurry her two younger children along, finally picking Edward up with one arm while clinging to Eleanor's hand with the other. Soon the crowd became too much, and Eleanor was swept away. The air grew intensely hot as Mildred and Edward tried to get through the throng, looking for Eleanor as they were shoved along toward the exit. Edward was having trouble breathing. He told his mother he wanted to lie down and go to sleep. Soon after, both Edward and Mildred lost consciousness.

On the other side of the tent, people tried to escape out the northeast and northwest exits, but when the fire broke out the crew hadn't finished removing the animal chutes. The only way to escape here now was to clamber up the four-foot-high cages, over the frightened, dangerous cats. At least six were still in the chutes when the fire broke out.

At first, circus staff tried to prevent people from exiting the tent this way, for fear that the cats would attack if someone's arm or leg slipped between the bars of the chute. However, fire proved the more fearsome enemy, and many people who escaped by this route might have perished otherwise.

Donalda La Voie remembers being terrified while climbing over the chute. The steel cage seemed very high as she inched across on her hands and knees. The cats were still beneath her, and Donalda feared she'd fall between the bars. For a second, she got stuck. "My foot kind of slipped, and I yanked it out." Finally across, she and her uncle and brother got away through a hole in the tent at the end of the chute.

Morris Handler and his three-year-old son, Phil, escaped over a chute too. Morris put Phil on his back and climbed up onto the metal cage. Once they were over the top and on the other side, they found the area blocked by circus wagons parked up against the side of the tent. Morris put his son on the ground in front of him, and together they squeezed under the wagons. There were people all around, struggling through the same tight spot. As they crawled to safety, Morris yelled, "Let my little boy through!"

Finally, performers May Kovar and Joseph Walsh were able to push their animals through the chutes and into their cages. Every one of the animals made it out of the tent unharmed. As the situation inside the big top grew dire, May helped people, especially children, climb over the chutes to safety.

After seeing his seven-year-old son David safely across a chute, William Curlee stayed inside the tent, pushing people over to the other side. William was 29 years old and a strong man. He refused to leave when he knew he could still help those who were too weak or scared to climb the bars of the chutes on their own. "People couldn't get past, so he stood there and got his

The big top about to collapse.

son, women, children, and others and pushed them over [the chutes]," William's sister Barbara Rubenthaler told a reporter years later. As the tent began to give way, William braved falling burning ropes and canvas. He helped many people escape before a nearby tent pole gave way and fell on him. William Curlee died a hero.

The big top was now engulfed in flames, and it looked like it was about to fall completely. Despite the danger, some who had gotten out safely tried to re-enter the tent to look for their loved ones. Police officers restrained them, knowing there was little chance of a second escape.

Hartford police officer Daniel McAuliffe was stationed inside the tent. As he was helping people off the bleachers, a man dropped a child down into his arms. The man then jumped down himself, holding another child. "Some dirty son of a bitch tossed or dropped a cigarette," the man told McAuliffe before he and his children disappeared into the crowd.

When the fire came to a roaring pitch, bandleader Merle Evans finally gave the signal for his group to grab their instruments and run. They had remained on the bandstand, opposite from where the fire had started, playing as long as they could. Once outside, the band regrouped and, in a small but sincere attempt to calm the frightened crowd, played on.

The fire had been blazing for only 10 minutes when the mighty big top collapsed in a rush of flames and screams. There were still people trapped inside.

# "THE DAY THE CLOWNS CRIED"

---

*"Tumult and wild disorder spread over the circus lot. Dishevelled women, without shoes, with torn stockings, roamed over the grounds calling for their children."*
—Hartford Times, July 6, 1944 *(extra edition)*

---

The first fire alarm went off at 2:44 PM, but it was already too late. Because the canvas roof of the tent had been waterproofed with a mixture of paraffin wax and gasoline, it was extremely flammable. When the fire began, this coating turned the tent into a giant candle, and it melted to the ground before fire trucks even arrived on the scene.

Aerial view of the destroyed big top.

The circus grounds were in chaos. Survivors wandered around in a daze. People were crying and frantically searching for their loved ones. The *Hartford Courant* reported that "one woman, who was joined by a man, knelt down in prayer. In a few minutes the woman's two children, faces smudged and clothes torn, came out of the crowd and ran to her arms."

Alden B. Crandall helped the rescue effort by carrying stretchers away from the tent, all the while keeping an eye out for his missing son. "I went back to my car with my wife and the other kids," he told the *Providence Journal*. "They were all crying, and I was too. The darn fool kid was there in the backseat, waiting for us. 'Daddy,' and he was bawling. 'I thought you were dead. I climbed through the bleacher and ran to the car—you always said to go to the car if we were separated.'"

Donald Cook wandered around the circus grounds, looking for his mother, brother, and sister. He couldn't find them. A couple from Hartford noticed Donald was alone and took him to their home to keep him safe. They gave him something to eat and called the police so his family would know he had survived. Today we might fear the thought of strangers taking a child home with them. But communities were closer then, and many children were cared for by strangers in the aftermath of the disaster.

When Eugene Badger and his father got out of the tent, they were sad to see many people who had been badly burned. "We saw a woman come running out of the tent. She was smoldering," Eugene recalled. Someone helped the woman extinguish the flames by rolling her on the ground, and then they picked her up and took her to get help.

As the Badgers walked home, Eugene's mother was riding on the city bus. She had left the Red Cross as soon as she heard about the fire. Amazingly, she spotted her husband and son through the window. She no doubt felt enormous relief when she saw that they were both all right.

Circus performers, while hurrying to haul water and help injured people, were devastated. They felt a special connection to their audiences. They wanted to make people smile and laugh. Instead, their beloved circus had brought tears and pain.

For days after, survivors praised the quick thinking and kindness of the Ringling Bros. workers. "The circus people were wonderful," Charles Comp told a *Hartford Courant* reporter. "The band played until the musicians had to jump to safety, the ushers stood at their sections assisting the panic-stricken crowd, and the performers did everything they could."

Survivor Helen Hathaway also commended the circus performers when she spoke to a reporter at the city's other major newspaper in the 1940s, the *Hartford Times*. "They were so calm that they prevented panic by their attitude."

Photographer Ralph Emerson captured a picture of Emmett Kelly—his clown makeup melted, his tramp costume charred—carrying a bucket of water across the field. It was to become the most famous photograph of the disaster. People would remember July 6, 1944, as "the day the clowns cried."

Unlike the previous tragic circus fire, all the animals survived the fire in Hartford. Animal handlers yelled, "Tails!" and the elephants lined up, trunk to tail, to be led onto Barbour Street, away from the blaze. Trainers tied up some of the smaller animals to any available post or tree outside the tent. The *Boston Globe* reported, "The circus animals were comparatively quiet during the fire, which handlers considered especially remarkable inasmuch as many of them had gone through the 1942 circus fire at Cleveland."

The Wallendas, who had helped many audience members escape the tent, could not find their little daughter, Carla. Panicked, they looked for her everywhere. Helen thought Carla had been watching the show from the audience, and she feared the worst. It turned out Carla had been playing outside the tent with the daughter of another performer when the fire broke out. The two girls had been led away from the tent during the chaos. Finally, police connected with the Wallendas to let them know that Carla was safely in their care.

Emmett Kelly helps during the disaster.

The Flying Wallendas (the little girl is probably Carla).

Firefighters hosing down the burned remains of the big top discovered young Elliot Smith by the animal chutes. He had fallen in the crowd, and as people tripped and fell on top of him, he was crushed beneath the weight of their bodies—but also somewhat protected from the flames. When the firefighters reached Elliot, they carefully lifted him up and carried him to a car that would take him to the hospital.

Donald Gale, another survivor, was found near the center ring, with his chameleon still in his pocket. The chameleon died in the intense heat of the fire, but Donald didn't. Like Elliot, he was protected by the unfortunate people who had fallen on top of him.

Brothers Guy and Jeff Cummings, fourteen and four years old the time of the fire, lived in a tight-knit community in East Hartford called Hillstown. Most folks there were farmers, and people looked after one another and each other's kids. "It was an ideal time for kids growing up," Guy recalled. "There wasn't really anything to scare you or threaten you." After the circus fire, five people from their small neighborhood never came home.

With the destruction of the circus, many of the hired hands were out of a job, including the teenager who had run away from home, Robert Segee. At first, Robert hung around because he had no money and no place to go. Then a few days later, word made it to his parents that their son was in Hartford. They sent bus fare, and Robert headed home to Portland, Maine, leaving the circus behind him.

It would soon become clear that both the city of Hartford and the Ringling Bros. circus had not done

Nicholas Zaccaro and Leo Goodman look at the wreckage of the big top.

enough to prevent the fire. But because of the war, Hartford was more than prepared to deal with the disaster. Fears of an invasion or bombing by the Germans had caused the city of Hartford, as well as many other cities across the United States, to make plans in case of an emergency. On July 6, auxiliary firefighters, police, and thousands of civilian defense volunteers were thrown into action. Trucks from local businesses were ready to help carry the wounded to hospitals. The Hartford Coca-Cola distributor, for example, sent seven trucks filled with stretchers.

Police officers responded to the first sounding of the fire alarm. They directed traffic away from the scene and kept onlookers from the area. They helped injured people into trucks and ambulances. At headquarters downtown, officers made phone calls to area funeral homes and hospitals to alert them of the victims being brought in.

"We were repairing a meter on the corner of Pearl and Ann Sts., when the fire alarm sounded," Sergeant Weinstein, Officer Dooley, and Officer Donahue wrote in a witness statement. "We immediately drove to the circus grounds. . . . At once, we commenced to assist in the removing of the bodies from the afflicted area to a clearing. We then secured a large canvas bag from a nearby circus wagon and into it we placed all the

Police officers and nurses were among those at the scene
immediately following the fire.

articles we could salvage which might later be used for identification purposes."

Units from the state national guard, the army, and the navy all came to the aid of the city. The Red Cross had recruited so many volunteer nurses that 150 who had reported for duty were sent home. Countless people from the surrounding neighborhoods and nearby towns helped the rescue efforts in any way they could. The governors of Massachusetts and Vermont also offered aid; they were graciously thanked, but their help was unneeded.

Later, in a radio address, Connecticut Governor Raymond Baldwin mentioned by name and thanked the countless organizations that volunteered their help during the crisis. "We can be intensely proud of the spirit with which the people of Connecticut met the emergency," said Governor Baldwin. "There are heroes, nameless and innumerable, in this tragedy."

The Red Cross had collected thousands of pints of blood during the war. Though the East Coast was never attacked, the blood was put to good use helping the hundreds of people who had been injured in the fire. When the supply seemed to be running out, a "request for Type O blood met with one hundred offers in just a few hours." By the time the crisis was over, the Red Cross had spent $83,159 to help the circus fire victims. This included more than $40,000 collected by the *Hartford Times* and $16,000 contributed by the Ringling Bros. circus.

One problem the city encountered was communication among police officers and others dealing with the disaster. According to the *Hartford Courant*, "Telephone service throughout Greater Hartford was disrupted by news of the fire as thousands of residents, office workers, and others near telephones rushed to spread the story or to find out if friends or relatives had escaped the flames."

There were no telephones on the circus grounds, but members of the Boy Scouts served as messengers between emergency personnel. Officers who needed to call headquarters had to use the phones in nearby homes. Some residents were anxious to help anyone in need. Survivors lined up on the porches of neighboring houses, hoping the owners would be kind enough to let them place a call. Harry Lichtenbaum, age 13, and his married sister, Doris, knocked on the door of a house on Barbour Street and were welcomed in to use the phone. They called their mother, who had no idea what was going on at the circus grounds. "Mom, we're all right!" Doris said. "Of course you're all right," her mother responded. "What do you mean? What has happened? Has something gone wrong?"

Others in the neighborhood saw an opportunity to make a profit. One house charged a quarter a call, and another requested as much as five dollars for people to call home. A woman in a nearby apartment put up a sign in her window saying TELEPHONE. She charged the long line of frightened survivors a dollar each to call their families.

The radio was an important source of information for people anxiously wondering if someone they knew had been caught in the blaze. The comforting but firm voice of the announcer repeatedly told listeners that they should remain calm and that "hysteria will only add to the confusion." Those with missing family members were urged to call the Connecticut War Council at phone number "Hartford 7-0181," where someone would take down their information and help them locate their loved ones.

There were three places people could look. Lost children had been rounded up by the police and led to the Brown School on Market Street. There, Officer Ella Brown and others played with the children on the playground and fed them cookies and lemonade. It was after midnight by the time all the children had finally been claimed by relatives or friends. Many of the kids didn't realize how devastating the disaster had been.

The next place to look was one of the local hospitals. The largest number of injured people were taken to Municipal Hospital because it was closest to the circus grounds. Other patients were sent to St. Francis Hospital or Hartford Hospital, some distance away.

A girl is reunited with a family member at the Brown School.

The last place anyone wanted to look for family was at the State Armory on Broad Street. This huge stone building housed weapons and ammunition and served as a training ground for soldiers preparing to leave for the war. On July 6, it became a morgue. There were more deaths than the hospitals could handle, so the bodies of people who had died were brought to the armory. There, people were let in to try to identify their kin among the rows of bodies laid out on cots.

In all, 167 people died, and 487 people were hospitalized. Of those who perished, 59 were children under 10 years old.

# 5

# MUNICIPAL HOSPITAL

---

*"We had two hands and did whatever we could to save steps for those whose experience and ability was most needed elsewhere."*

—volunteer nurse's aide Patricia Wakefield, Hartford Courant, *July 7, 1944 (morning edition)*

---

T he cries of burn victims echoed through the corridors of Municipal Hospital. Some patients lay on gurneys in the middle of the hallways, and others filled chairs in the waiting room. Hundreds of injured people and their relatives waited their turn to see the doctors.

Throughout the disaster, doctors and nurses at all three of Hartford's hospitals did everything they could to care for their patients and, in many cases, they saved their lives. Volunteers played an important role too. They made beds, rolled bandages, applied dressings, passed out cups of juice, and comforted victims.

When new patients arrived at Municipal Hospital, nurses rushed the worst cases into operating rooms to receive treatment. There, doctors cut off their charred clothes, covered them with cool, sterile sheets, and gave them a drug called morphine to dull the pain. Burns were covered with salve and then wrapped in gauze. Nurses hooked up an IV that sent healthy, new blood into the patients' veins. Finally, patients were given penicillin to prevent infection. This was important because their immune systems were already busy working to repair the burned skin, making it difficult for their bodies to also fight off germs.

One of the biggest problems for the hospitals was the sheer number of patients. There simply weren't enough doctors and nurses to see everyone. A call for help went out to all medical professionals in the area, and it was answered almost immediately. Nurses from the city's large insurance companies volunteered, and doctors from neighboring towns came too. Medical examiner William J. Brickley, a burn expert from Boston, came to help treat the victims. He brought a team of three men: a medical examiner and two mortuary assistants.

These men had helped patients after a nightclub fire in Boston that had claimed 492 lives and left countless victims of severe burns. They used their experience from that disaster to help hospital workers give the circus fire patients the best possible treatment.

Everyone worked into the night, fighting exhaustion as they treated patient after patient. Hartford Hospital, the largest in the city, saw 51 patients. Doctors and nurses at the smaller Municipal Hospital saw nearly triple that number. Within the first hours after the fire, they treated 143 patients for burns and other injuries, many of them critical. By eight o'clock that night, too tired to work anymore, the first shift of medical personnel was sent home to rest. Mary Sullivan, the hospital superintendent, begged volunteers to come back after they'd had some sleep. "Please all of you . . . all of you who can come back tonight, please do. I think we are going to need everybody we can get."

Fire victims bravely faced their injuries. "People as a whole were well behaved; there was no complaining even from those who were severely hurt. Small children, their skins charred with burns, tried to smile at us," nurse's aide Patricia Wakefield of Municipal Hospital told the *Hartford Courant.*

It would have been nearly impossible for the hospitals to help as many people as they did without the generosity of the nurses, doctors, and others who volunteered their time and knowledge. Fifteen-year-old Shirley Lawton and her best friend Dot were "a couple of pinkies" (the nickname used for young hospital volunteers). The two had escaped the fire themselves, only to find the terrible sights in the halls of Hartford Hospital when they reported for duty. "We had a hard

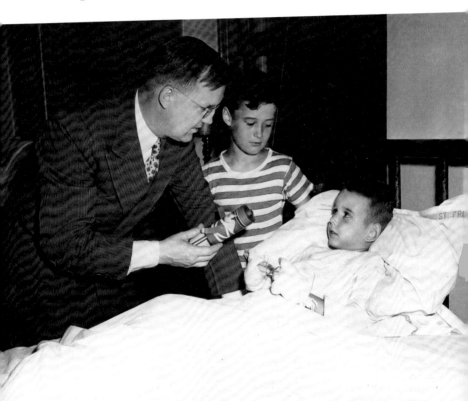

The mayor of Hartford gives a toy to five-year-old Robert Hopkins Jr., who had been burned in the fire. Beside him is Donald MacRae, age 12, who had escaped unhurt.

time getting off that day," Shirley said. "The head nurse didn't want to let us off. It was just a horror."

Just a comforting word was enough to keep some patients going. Some of the children had lost siblings and parents, so nurses often played the roles of both caregiver and mother. It must have been incredibly frightening for the many small children being treated at the hospitals, including those who were unaware of the circus fire.

Five-year-old Kenneth Sinkwitz hadn't been to the circus, but he arrived at St. Francis Hospital in Hartford just a few days after the fire to have his tonsils removed. "I'll never forget the children screaming," he said. "I didn't know what was going on until I asked the nurse." The hospital was crowded and noisy. Nurses and doctors hurried up and down the halls checking on their patients.

After the fire had been put out, a rescue worker had found eight-year-old Jerry LeVasseur by one of the animal chutes. Jerry had suffered many injuries, and he needed help immediately. Unconscious when he arrived at the hospital, Jerry woke up to find himself enclosed in a kind of tent where machines pumped oxygen all around him. This made his blood carry more oxygen to his cells, helping him to recover. The doctors and nurses watched over him carefully, and eventually his body healed. In June 1945, after 11 months at Municipal Hospital, Jerry finally went home.

Elliot Smith, who had also been found by one of the animal chutes, was with Jerry at Municipal Hospital. While he was recovering from his burns, Elliot

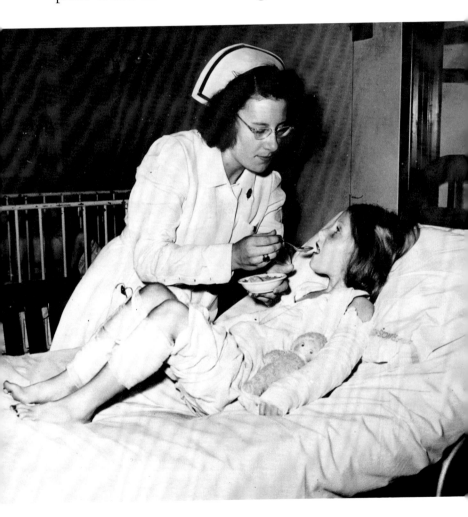

**Nurse Phyllis Willet takes care of Marie Ann Connors.**

developed pneumonia, a common complication for burn patients. Elliot never forgot undergoing skin grafts to cover the areas where he was most badly burned. "Those were the worst times," he said in a Connecticut Public Television documentary. But he also has some happy memories, including the times when the kids at the hospital ran through the corridors playing hide-and-seek. The nurses had to chase them back into bed.

While he was at the hospital, Elliot kept an autograph book where his friends and nurses signed their names and wrote messages. It's easy to see from their cheerful notes that the kids still knew how to have a little fun.

Barbara Smith wrote:

Remember the girl from the city.
Remember the girl from the town.
Remember the Girl that spoiled this book by writing upside down.

And Jimmie Sullivan wrote:

Roses are red and
violets are blue
God made me beautiful
but wha' happen to you?

Elliot spent his eighth birthday at the hospital and went home in late November.

Donald Gale was admitted to Municipal Hospital with severe burns and, like Jerry LeVasseur, was immediately put into an oxygen tent. Like Elliot, he also developed pneumonia. Donald recovered from his injuries, but it took a long time for his body to heal. Almost a year after the fire Donald, Jerry, and six-year-old Patty Murphy were the last children to leave the hospital.

Mildred and Edward Cook were carried from the scene of the fire and brought to Municipal Hospital. Both were severely burned. Doctors treated Mildred's burns and wrapped her body in gauze. They wanted to move her to the less crowded Hartford Hospital; however, they didn't want to separate her from her son. Edward was still breathing, but just barely.

Hearing news of the fire, Mildred's family in Southampton was worried. They hadn't heard from Mildred, and they knew she had planned to take the children to the circus. Mildred's brother, Ted Parsons, and her sister, Emily (Parsons) Gill, rushed to Hartford, fearing the worst.

Of course no one was home when they arrived at Mildred's apartment. Ted stayed behind in case the telephone rang, and Emily set off to find Mildred and her children. First, she went to the Brown School, where

Patty Murphy celebrates Christmas in the hospital.

she learned that Mildred had been taken to Municipal Hospital. Emily raced to her sister's side and discovered her nephew Edward was also there.

Meanwhile, Ted's wife, Marion, arrived in Hartford accompanied by a family friend, the Reverend James Yee. They met Ted at the apartment and waited for news from Emily. Not long after, there was a knock on the door. It was Donald. The kind couple that had taken care of him after the tragedy had fed him dinner and brought him home. Ted and Marion must have felt tremendous relief when they hugged their nephew close and saw that he was unharmed.

Later that evening, they all went to meet Emily at the hospital. Their visit with Mildred was short. She was groggy from medications, and her face was wrapped in gauze. In another room, they visited Edward. He was very weak, but he asked about his mother and sister. After a few minutes, it was time to go, and Donald said good-bye to his brother. They never saw each other again. Edward died the next night.

Donald was safe in the comforting arms of his aunts and uncle. Doctors and nurses cared for Mildred at Municipal Hospital, and Edward had gone to a place where pain could no longer touch him. But where was Donald's sister, Eleanor? This question would haunt the people of Hartford for nearly 50 years.

# 6

# "WHO KNOWS THIS CHILD?"

*"Into the big drill shed, hastily established as a morgue for persons who died in the fire, filed a long line of silent men and women."*

—Hartford Times, *July 6, 1944 (extra edition)*

The line of people outside the State Armory snaked around the side of the huge stone edifice. The building included a cavernous drill shed—a giant room with three-story-high ceilings—where members of the National Guard practiced for combat. This room is where the makeshift morgue was set up for 145 bodies waiting to be identified after the fire.

The faces of those in line were anxious. Some people cried quietly. Others stood in a kind of stupor. The *Boston Globe* reported that "some were so stricken by the sudden disaster they did not even turn their heads when asked questions. Some looked blankly at persons who addressed them as if they could not summon their senses to answer." It was eerily quiet. But the *Hartford Courant* reported that there was also an air of hope. Though strangers, the people standing in line helped each other to stay positive. They reminded each other that there was still a chance that a wife, husband, or child was merely lost and not lying among the bodies inside. For many, it was a long night. Women from the War Council's Rolling Kitchen brought sandwiches and coffee to the people in line. They offered consoling words to soothe aching hearts.

Between late afternoon and midnight on the day of the fire, 2,500 people came to view the bodies at the armory. On the radio, announcers spoke calmly and clearly, instructing people to "please stay away from the armory and scene of the accident if no one is missing from your home." Curiosity seekers could get in the way, and families needed space to grieve. Military troops and police patrolled the area. Only people looking to find their relatives were allowed near.

Inside the armory, volunteers did all they could to help families identify their loved ones as quickly as possible, sparing them from looking at more bodies than absolutely necessary. They organized the bodies on cots in rows by age and sex as best they could and covered them with blankets. Men, women, and children were placed in separate sections, with the most recognizable bodies lined up in front.

Medical personnel inspected each body and wrote down any identifying marks. They noted hair color, eye color, and any clothing or jewelry the victim was

Outside the Connecticut State Armory.

wearing. Even the smallest detail could help identify a body. E. J. O'Connell was able to pick out his five-year-old daughter, Doris Jean, by a bandage tucked in her curled fist. He had wrapped it around her finger when she had hurt it just that morning. Another family identified their daughter by a scrap of cloth from her bright sundress that still clung to her body. Sometimes there were few clues to go by. Many bodies were burned beyond recognition.

A nurse and a police officer accompanied each person who walked up and down the aisles of cots. The nurse compared notes taken on the body with the description given by the family member. If the details matched, the police officer lifted the blanket. While many people amazingly kept their composure, others were overwhelmed with emotion when they saw the body and then had to say whether or not it was the person they were seeking.

After E. J. O'Connell had identified both his wife and daughter, one of the rescue workers approached him. "I was the one who found this child. If it can be of any comfort to you, there was an adult lying on top with arms around her." Doris Jean's mother had protected her as best she could. Another woman searching for her daughter approached the line of cots with reddened eyes. She found her daughter's body in a far corner of the giant room. With no tears left to weep, she took one last look at her little girl and said, simply, "So long as I know."

Even those who had experience dealing with disasters found the scene hard to take in. A policeman stationed at the armory told a *Boston Globe* reporter, "I've been a cop for 25 years, but I never saw anything like this. I won't sleep for weeks. And I was gonna take my kid to the circus today. But I had to work. Thank God. I had to work."

Outside the armory, a radio car announced over its loudspeaker the names of missing persons who had been found at one of the hospitals and the children who remained unclaimed at the Brown School. Some people burst into tears when they heard their relative had been found alive. These small miracles gave hope to those left standing anxiously in line.

One of the unidentified bodies inside the armory was that of a little girl whose light-brown curly hair framed her face. Her injuries showed that she'd probably been trampled in the rush to get out of the tent. She had a burn mark on one cheek, her forehead was swollen, and her mouth had been damaged, but unlike many of the bodies that surrounded her, her face was recognizable. She still looked like someone's little girl.

Medical examiner Dr. Walter Weissenborn took down her information: a white female, about six years of age; blue eyes; shoulder-length, light-brown curly hair; 3 feet 10 inches tall; approximate weight, 40 pounds. He noted on a dental chart that the child had two permanent teeth, incisors, on the bottom of her mouth. The rest were baby teeth (dentists call them deciduous teeth). She wore a flowered dress and brown shoes. Dr. Weissenborn gave the unidentified girl a number—1565. The volunteers at the armory thought surely this little girl would be one of the first to be claimed.

When Emily Gill did not find Eleanor Cook at the Brown School or the hospital, she decided to go to the armory. She had to face the very real possibility that her missing niece was dead. Emily gave the attendants a description of Eleanor, and the nurses on duty felt a surge of hope. Light-brown hair, blue eyes—the description seemed to match the little girl tagged 1565. A nurse and a police escort led Emily slowly through the rows of cots. The responsibility of identifying her niece weighed heavily on her shoulders.

The escort pulled back the army blanket to reveal the young face of 1565. Emily took a long look at the little girl. She thought it might be Eleanor, but she wasn't sure. The examination chart said that this little girl had two permanent teeth and was 3 feet 10 inches tall. Emily was sure that Eleanor had eight permanent upper teeth. The height didn't seem to match either. Eleanor was eight years old, and everyone in the family agreed that she was tall for her age. At 3 feet 10 inches, this little girl's height was closer to that of a six-year-old.

Eleanor Cook.

Emily told the attendants that this little girl was not Eleanor.

Later, Marion and Ted Parsons and Reverend James Yee visited the armory to look for Eleanor. The attendants took the anxious group straight to the little girl tagged 1565. But Marion knew right away that it wasn't Eleanor, whom she had raised and loved as a daughter.

This little girl had shoulder-length hair. Eleanor's hair was cut short.

This little girl was wearing a white flowered dress and brown shoes. Marion had packed a red playsuit for Eleanor to wear to the circus. Furthermore, Eleanor did not own a dress or shoes like the ones on this little girl.

This little girl had only two permanent teeth. Eleanor had eight permanent teeth: four on the top and four on the bottom. (Not eight on the top, as Emily had said earlier.)

Marion Parsons, so close to her niece that Eleanor had called her Mom, said no, she was certain it was not Eleanor. Ted and James Yee agreed.

Eleanor's family looked at all the girls who remained unidentified, including a girl with the morgue number 1503. According to an examination by Dr. Weissenborn, she was approximately nine years old, and she had eight permanent teeth. However, the body had been so badly burned it would be impossible for anyone to recognize her. None of the other girls remaining at the armory matched Eleanor's description.

Back at Mildred's apartment, the family was devastated. They were exhausted from anxiety and sorrow. Somehow, they had to pull themselves together and figure out what to do next. Ted and Marion decided to drive Donald back to Southampton to take care of him and to plan his brother Edward's funeral. Emily volunteered to stay in Hartford. She'd keep an eye on Mildred and continue to look for Eleanor. Ted and Marion scooped up their nephew and, with James Yee, got into the car and drove away, leaving Hartford behind.

As the hours passed, it seemed more and more unlikely that Eleanor was simply missing. Emily inquired back at the armory a second time. There were no new bodies, the attendants told her. The only little girl matching Eleanor's description was the one she'd seen before, the one tagged 1565.

Emily agreed to look at the body again. She felt conflicted. True, this girl had light-brown hair and blue eyes, but Emily could not get past the teeth. They looked wrong, and there were only two permanent ones according to the dental chart that accompanied the body. The attendants asked Emily to have Eleanor's dentist send an X-ray for comparison, but it was not to be. Sadly, the Cook family dentist was on vacation out of the country and could not be reached. Without the dental records, there was no clear proof, and Emily again told the nurses that this little girl was not Eleanor. This bit of unlucky timing would shadow the identification of 1565 for some time to come. The issue of her teeth would become one of the most contentious in the identification of the little girl.

On the evening of July 7, police commissioner Edward Hickey assigned state trooper Sam Freeman to help Emily in her search. Together they visited all the funeral homes in the area that had bodies of little girls about Eleanor's age who had died in the fire. Maybe someone had taken Eleanor's body by mistake? By the end of the night, they'd gone to six funeral homes and still had not found Eleanor.

Emily returned to Mildred's apartment to rest, while Officer Freeman, armed with a photograph of Eleanor, worked through the night to find the missing girl. The next day, he showed the photo to a nurse's aide and a social worker at Municipal Hospital who had cared for 1565 before she had died. He also showed Eleanor's photo to some policemen at the armory and to Dr. Weissenborn. They all believed that Eleanor resembled the little girl numbered 1565.

Freeman thought he had solved the mystery. He asked Emily to come to Hartford Hospital, where the body of 1565 was now being held, to make an identification. Emily saw the body yet again and, according to Freeman's report, claimed, "This was the one that she had looked at at the Hartford Armory with her brother. The only thing that made her say that this was not Eleanor, was the fact that she thought Eleanor had 8 second upper teeth, whereas this body had four second upper teeth and four second lower teeth. She said that if it hadn't been for that, she would say that the child was her niece, Eleanor Cook."

Again, there was confusion about the teeth. Freeman's report states 1565 had four upper and four lower permanent teeth; however, the dental chart prepared by one of the medical examiners listed 1565 as having only two permanent teeth. Was the dental chart wrong? Or was Freeman? Could Freeman have been accidentally referring to the other unidentified girl, 1503, a child with eight permanent teeth? There is a curious note written on the dental chart for 1503, made on July 9, after Freeman's inquiry. It says, "Neighborhood dentist in Southampton, Mass. gone." The medical examiner who had X-rayed the teeth of 1503 and created the chart had made a note about Eleanor, despite the fact that no one had connected 1503 with her. Could the examiners have accidentally switched the morgue numbers when they filled out the charts? In any case, Emily still would not confirm that 1565 was her niece. The search was officially ended when she wrote the following letter to the police commissioner.

Dear Mr. Hickey: I wish to thank you for my family and me for your help and cooperation in our search for my niece, Eleanor Cook. I would like to thank you also for letting us have Trooper Freeman of Colchester Barracks to help us. He was very kind and very efficient in checking and re-checking all the clues we could get. We took the names of the little girls her age who had been identified and checked at the funeral homes in case of misidentity. We checked the little girl at Municipal Hospital who answered to Eleanor's description and found her to be the "mystery" girl, whom we know definitely is not she. Because the figures are 6 unidentified and 6 missing we felt she must be misidentified. However, she might never have left the tent. God alone knows. Again I thank you for your help in our sorrow.

Sincerely, (Mrs.) Emily Parsons Gill

Those close to Eleanor—Emily Gill, Ted and Marion Parsons, and James Yee—all saw the body of 1565.

None of them thought the little girl was their Eleanor. But what about Mildred Cook? Wouldn't she know for certain if this unidentified little girl was her daughter? Unfortunately, Mildred never saw the body of 1565. She was in a coma for several weeks after the disaster, long past the time all the funerals had been held. In the months and years after the fire, Mildred's family shielded her from any news of the tragedy. Mildred and Donald eventually moved to Southampton with Ted and Marion. No one ever showed Mildred the pictures of the unidentified little girl that had appeared in newspapers across the country for many years after the fire. Mildred grieved the loss of her dearly loved children Eleanor and Edward and accepted the fact that her daughter's body would never be found.

If 1565 was not Eleanor Cook, who was she? Why had no one claimed the little girl with the curly light-brown hair? Had everyone else in her family died in the fire? Was she a runaway? The rumors flew. But there was another possibility that could very well be true.

In the days after the fire, parents coming to the armory to claim the bodies of their children were understandably distraught. Was it possible that a parent had claimed the wrong child?

Many people were in a hurry to find their relatives. At the time, Hartford had a large Jewish population.

Those who were strict observers of the faith needed to bury their dead by sundown according to Jewish law. Was it possible that in the urgency to find their children, people could have taken the wrong bodies?

In the end, 1565 wasn't the only body that was never claimed. The stack of coroner's reports was thick. These single sheets of paper captured the last details of the lives of 167 people. Six of those pages began with the words "An Unknown." Three adults, one boy, the girl 1503, and the girl 1565 remained unidentified. All except 1565 had been so severely burned that they were impossible to identify.

On July 12, 1944, the *Hartford Times* ran 1565's morgue photo in the paper. The headline asked local readers, WHO KNOWS THIS CHILD? It seems no one did.

The people of Hartford were so heartbroken over the sad story of the little girl that the city adopted her as one of their own. She was laid to rest in Northwood Cemetery on July 10, 1944, along with the bodies of the other unidentified victims. A stone slab was set in place to remind visitors of the tragedy and its unknown victims. The inscription reads,

**This plot of ground consecrated by the city of Hartford as a resting place for three adults and three children who lost their lives in the circus**

fire July 6, 1944. Their identity known but to God.

Behind the stone, six small white markers list morgue numbers 1503, 1510, 2019, 2200, and 4512. The sixth marker is specially inscribed, "Little Miss 1565."

# 7

# WHO WAS TO BLAME?

---

*"Seven officials and employees of the Ringling Brothers and Barnum and Bailey Combined Shows, Inc., were held criminally responsible . . . for Hartford's disastrous circus fire last July 6."*

—Hartford Courant, *January 12, 1945*

---

I n the days and months after the Hartford circus fire, people gathered their families and friends close. They hugged their neighbors who had come home safe and unharmed. They visited patients in the hospitals. They planned and attended funerals. One memory that stands out among the people who lived through the fire is how everyone in the community supported each other during the bad times.

The citizens of Hartford took care of one another, but had the managers of the Ringling Bros. circus cared for the safety of their guests when they beckoned them to come see "The Greatest Show On Earth"? And what about the city of Hartford? Did the city have an obligation to the people who had come from down the street and across the state to see the circus? Fingers pointed at both Ringling Bros. and Hartford, but who was to blame?

In the 1940s, fires were not uncommon at circuses. At that time, many people smoked, and a carelessly thrown match or cigarette could easily start a fire on the hay strewn on the ground for the animals, especially if the weather had been very dry. Usually, circuses were well prepared to quickly extinguish any fires that might pop up. Unfortunately, in Hartford, the Ringling Bros. circus did not follow proper safety procedures.

An investigation by the Hartford Board of Inquiry revealed the following:

- Not enough circus staff were on hand to fight the fire.
- The nearest fire hydrant was 300 feet from the main entrance, and the circus's fire hoses did not fit the city hydrants.

- Only 24 buckets of water, and no fire extinguishers, were placed throughout the tent.
- The steel animal chutes blocked two of the main exits.
- Staff had failed to post No Smoking signs inside the main tent.

Police Commissioner Hickey also reported that the big top tent had been waterproofed with a highly flammable mixture of 1,800 pounds of wax and 6,000 gallons of gasoline. We might be shocked by this method of waterproofing today, but it was common practice at the time. The Ringling Bros. circus had treated the canvas big top the same way for a number of years before the fire. John Ringling North, then a director on the board of the Ringling Bros. and Barnum & Bailey Combined Shows, Inc., claimed that he had tried to obtain fireproof tents in 1944. However, North said, the government denied access to these tents because such specialty supplies were reserved for the war effort.

Years later, a report by Henry Cohn, a lawyer for the state of Connecticut, confirmed that "the armed forces had exclusive control of the only proven flame-retardant waterproofing solvent for use on their canvas tents." He goes on to note, "Other circuses claimed

Pieces of the curved steel animal chute can be seen in the foreground. A still-assembled chute can be seen in the background between two sections of the grandstand. Boxcars from the circus train also blocked that exit.

to have found equally satisfactory and safe treatments; the Ringlings later claimed to have tested the available chemicals and found they were quite flammable. Also when the tent was dragged to the next location, the solvent was easily scraped off." On the other hand in 1991, circus fire researcher and journalist Lynne Tuohy suggested that perhaps the Ringling Bros. circus simply didn't want to use the safer fireproof tents because they were heavier and required more time and manpower to set up.

It is surprising that the Ringling Bros. circus continued to use flammable tents, even when they'd had trouble with them before. Fires had caused great damage to the big top in 1910 and 1912, though no one died in these instances. Then there was the horrible fire in the animal menagerie tent in 1942. The frightening similarity between that fire and the one in Hartford was how the circus had waterproofed the tents—both with the mixture of wax and gasoline. The circus had not learned from its mistakes.

So what about the city of Hartford? Did it have a role in not preventing the disaster? Certainly the aftermath of the fire was handled with authority and efficiency. But why didn't anyone from the Hartford fire department notice the safety violations? The simple answer is that neither the fire department nor the police department were expected to do anything to make sure the circus was safe. In fact, the fire department was never officially told that the circus was in town.

When the circus got into town on July 5, it was not properly inspected. Because the circus train had arrived late, the grounds were not set up when Charles Hayes, the building inspector, arrived to check that safety precautions had been met. His inspection wasn't a requirement in Hartford, but it was customary to have someone check things out. Hayes returned later in the afternoon, but things still weren't quite ready. He claimed that since the circus had always complied with fire safety regulations in the past, he was sure this year would be no different. Because the setup was not complete when Hayes left the grounds, he had not checked the fire extinguishers or the fire hoses. He did not even check the tent to make sure all the exits were clear. Hayes gave the circus the go-ahead anyway.

Downtown, Police Chief Charles Hallissey issued the circus a permit to perform on the Barbour Street lot, even though he had not checked the safety of the circus grounds or the tents either. Hallissey hastily filled out the permit form, not even bothering to write the date, and in exchange received 50 free passes to the show.

While Connecticut did not require the local fire department to be present at public events, several police officers were assigned and stationed throughout the tent. Detectives Paul Beckwith, Edward Lowe, and Thomas Barber had been onsite, and they remained on the case for some time after the disaster as well. What began as a routine assignment turned into a massive disaster response operation.

The official report of the Hartford County coroner cleared the city from any blame. "The report finds no legal responsibility to inspect circuses placed upon city fire, police, or building departments." Instead, the entire blame for the disaster was placed upon the Ringling Bros. circus. Six circus officials were sent to jail because of the unsafe conditions inside the big top tent. On February 21, 1945, the men were found guilty of involuntary manslaughter.

Three circus officials were sentenced to one to five years in the state prison: James Haley, the circus's vice president and director, convicted for knowledge of unsafe conditions; general manager George W. Smith, convicted for negligence; and boss canvasman Leonard Aylesworth, who was in charge of supervising fire prevention, convicted for deliberately leaving his post and neglecting to appoint someone to supervise the fire equipment in his place. (On the day of the fire, Aylesworth was in Springfield, Massachusetts, preparing the next location.) Edward "Whitey" Versteeg, chief electrician, and William Caley, seat hand, were each sentenced to one year in prison; Versteeg for failing to distribute fire extinguishers and Caley for leaving his designated post. David Blanchfield, superintendent of rolling stock, was given six months for obstructing the tent's exits with his trucks. Some sentences were later reduced, but all six men served time in connection to the fire.

Ringling Bros. circus managers in court. Left to right: George W. Smith, James Haley, Edward "Whitey" Versteeg, Leonard Aylesworth, and David Blanchfield.

The Ringling Bros. and Barnum & Bailey Combined Shows, Inc. was ordered to pay $4 million to compensate people for their losses. Today that figure would be close to $42 million. It was a large enough sum to bankrupt the circus. Fortunately, the lawyers for the victims were clever. They arranged for the circus to continue to function because, they argued, if the circus were to close down, there would not be enough money to pay the damages owed to people. It was crucial that Ringling Bros. continue to put on their show. Incidentally, this plan worked out for the circus as well. It could be argued that if the lawyers had not come up with this plan, the Ringling Bros. and Barnum & Bailey Circus, the most popular circus in the United States, would not be around today.

William Caley began his prison sentence immediately, but the other convicted circus employees remained free long enough to help prepare for the upcoming 1945 spring season. A portion of the money earned each season would help pay the thousands of claims made by circus fire survivors and the families of the victims. Eventually, the Ringling Bros. circus paid every cent of that debt.

Regardless of who was to blame, many people wondered, could this kind of tragedy happen again? The mayor of Hartford decided to make some changes in how circuses and other outdoor events were handled by the city. Hartford became an example that other cities across the country would follow. In January 1945, officials passed a law that required careful inspections of events held in tents. The grounds, seats, aisles, exits, and first-aid facilities must be checked by police and fire departments. Smoking and overcrowding in the tents would not be allowed. All tents must be fireproof.

Officials also realized that every second counts when ambulances and fire trucks are on their way to an emergency. Before the circus fire, emergency vehicles did not always use their flashing lights to help them move quickly through traffic. Now, it was required for them to be on at all times.

Despite the new safety inspections, it was years before anyone in Hartford wanted to attend the circus again. As they grew older, survivors of the fire refused to take their children to circuses. Many had a lifelong fear of crowds. The Ringling Bros. circus performed in other cities in the years after the fire, but it did not return to Hartford again until 1975, more than 30 years later. By then, the circus was no longer performing inside a tent, but instead held its shows in indoor arenas.

Negligence on the part of both Ringling Bros. and the city of Hartford contributed to the tragedy. But was the fire, in fact, accidental? Was it possible that, when the seat hands left their stations to move the animal chutes, someone had intentionally put a match to the canvas?

**8**

# ACCIDENT OR ARSON?

---

*"An investigation of the cause, circumstances and origin of a fire which occurred in Hartford on July 6, 1944 during the circus performance at the Ringling Bros.—Barnum & Bailey Combined Shows, Inc. was instituted by me . . . to determine whether such fire was the result of carelessness or the act of an incendiary."*

—Report of Commissioner of State Police,
Edward J. Hickey, January 11, 1945

---

## – 1944 –

Arson was not foremost in the minds of the investigators as they walked through the charred remains of the big top in the days after the tragedy. Rumor spread that the cause of the fire was a cigarette or a match carelessly thrown onto dry grass covering the circus grounds or against the side wall of the tent. Police officer McAuliffe could not find the man who'd mentioned the cigarette to him. In McAuliffe's original report, he records the man's statement as "some dirty son of a bitch tossed or dropped a cigarette," which sounds more like the man was guessing than reporting something he had actually seen. In Commissioner Hickey's report, the statement is misquoted and sounds more accusing—"That dirty son-of-a-b---- just threw a cigarette butt!" The missing witness's remark could not be verified, but it had a huge impact. It was one of the things that led investigators to focus on an accidental cause instead of an intentional one.

Commissioner Hickey led a formal investigation after the fire. He leaned heavily on the cigarette theory. New York fire marshal Thomas Brophy, an expert in fire investigations, was called in. In his opinion, a carelessly dropped match or cigarette *could* have started the fire, but he also said he did not know the physical conditions at the time or whether there was any other flammable material near the location of the fire. He found that one of the wooden supports for the bleachers was badly charred at the bottom. A cigarette or match itself could not have ignited the support, but if the side wall of the tent was ignited first, it could have caused the support to catch fire. With so many variables and without a witness, Brophy could not make a definite conclusion.

Kenneth Gwinnell, an usher, made a statement to police in which he said it was common for cigarettes and discarded matches to start fires. He suggested that "a cigarette would have smoked for a while, but [the

Police detectives inspect the scene of the fire.

fire] came all of a sudden and it evidently was a match."
Whether it was the cigarette itself or the match used to
light it, Gwinnell's statement supported the idea that
the fire was accidental.

Commissioner Hickey defended his theory in an
interview with the Hartford County coroner, Frank E.
Healy.

> Coroner: "Supposing your chemical analysis of
> the side walls of that tent show that a cigarette
> under full force would not ignite that canvas?"
>
> Commissioner: "My answer to that would be
> based on the testimony before me, that consid-
> eration has got to be given to the dry ground,
> the condition of the ground, the manner in
> which the side wall canvas was hanging folded
> over on the ground, and the manner in which
> the cigarette or burned match landed on the
> combustible material."

Witnesses to the blaze, however, told a different
story. They reported that the fire had started high up
on the tent side wall, not on the ground. Jane Pelton,
age 12, said, "At about the end of the animal [act], just
as the animals were leaving the cage, someone shouted
help. I looked back to my right and saw a large flame

at the beginning of the roof of the tent." Helen Fyler, age 40, saw "a patch of flame about 6 or 8 feet wide at the point where the side wall meets the tent top." And Joseph Dewey, age 10, said, "I sat . . . about two seats from the top. While we were looking at the animals in the cage doing tricks, I heard someone say the tent was

This photo seems to show the origin of the fire, above the small tent that housed the men's restroom.

on fire. I looked back and I saw the fire where the tent bends over above the bleachers. This fire was just starting and there was a little hole in the tent. . . . I didn't see any fire along the bottom of the tent when we came out."

In fact, Commissioner Hickey contradicts himself when, in his own report, he notes, "Many patrons for the first time saw the fire burning the upper portion of the side wall canvas and the lower section of the top adjoining the side wall canvas."

Investigators from the Hartford police questioned and took statements from countless circus-goers and members of the Ringling Bros. staff. No one seemed to know how the fire started. A few employees had criminal records, and some were investigated on suspicion of arson. They were all dead ends.

Commissioner Hickey based his conclusions almost exclusively on the testimony of two men: Kenneth Gwinnell and Daniel McAuliffe. Neither man had actually seen how the fire started. Both of their statements relied on assumptions and hearsay.

Commissioner Hickey issued his final statement: "Upon the testimony before me, I find that this fire originated on the ground in the southwest end of the main tent back of the 'Blue Bleachers' about 50 feet south of the main entrance, and was so caused by the carelessness of an unidentified smoker and patron who threw a lighted cigarette to the ground from the 'Blue Bleachers' stand. The evidence before me does not disclose this to be the act of an incendiary."

The case was closed, and the cause of the Hartford circus fire was declared accidental . . . until six years later, when Robert Segee, the teenage member of the lighting crew, confessed to setting it.

Burned bleacher seats.

### – 1950 –

Now Segee was 20 years old, and he was in police custody on suspicion of setting a fire at a factory in Circleville, Ohio. As police detectives questioned him, the young man admitted to setting fires in Circleville and Columbus, Ohio, as well as in Portland, Maine. He also confessed to setting the circus fire in Hartford, Connecticut.

Commissioner Hickey was angry when he heard the news. It looked as though the police in Columbus, Ohio, were going to crack his case. What's more,

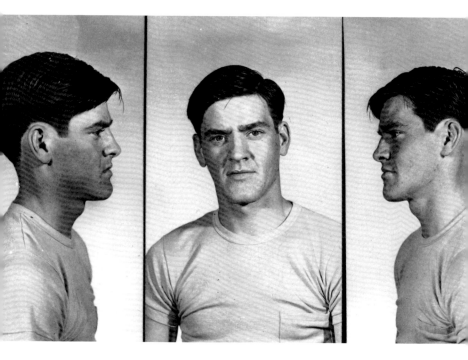

Robert Segee at age 20.

Hickey would look pretty bad if they revealed that he was wrong about the fire being an accident. Hickey sent police captains Paul Lavin and Paul Beckwith to Ohio to question Segee in relation to the Hartford fire, but when they arrived, authorities turned the investigators away. They said the reports were not written up yet, so they couldn't share their findings. Furthermore, the Hartford detectives could not interview Segee because the Circleville case was still open. In a letter to Commissioner Hickey, Lavin wrote: "It appeared throughout our investigation that these two gentlemen [Ohio detectives R. Russell Smith and LaMonda] want to get the credit of breaking the Hartford case as well as the cases in their own jurisdiction to build the prestige of their own office and division."

Commissioner Hickey was livid. In snappish back-and-forth phone calls and telegrams Hickey blamed authorities in Ohio for not sharing information about Robert Segee, and the Ohio authorities told Hickey to stay out of the way of their investigation.

Meanwhile, Ohio investigators pulled together details about Segee's past. They interviewed Robert's mother, Josephine Segee, and Dorothy Segee Thompson, his sister. According to Josephine, Robert's father "was always very mean to Robert. The boy was very sensitive and [he] would leave home every time his father would [holler] at him." Josephine told the investigators that as a child, Robert was afraid to go to bed because he was constantly plagued by bad dreams. At nine years old, Robert roamed the streets at night rather than face the nightmares. In the interview, Robert's mother said, "I never had any idea that Robert was setting any fires. I knew there was something wrong with him but you know how a mother is—I never wanted to admit it."

Dorothy, on the other hand, knew Robert had acted out in dangerous ways. She remembered her brother setting two fires at their house, one of which occurred when, at age five, Robert had thrown a newspaper onto an oil stove. Over the course of six years, 68 suspicious fires were reported within 10 blocks of the Segees' home. Could Robert have set those fires?

When Robert had joined the Ringling Bros. circus in June of 1944, perhaps he had hoped to escape his troubles. Instead, it appeared things had gotten worse.

Now, Ohio investigator R. Russell Smith and psychologist Dr. Bernard Higley interviewed Segee. During the interview, Segee described visions he'd had of a Native American he called "the red man." He said that this man had told him to start the fire at the circus in Hartford. Segee made several drawings during his mental evaluation. Most reflected his Native American heritage. Some were peaceful scenes: birds soaring over wooded landscapes; a man canoeing down a river. But Segee also drew pictures of his most disturbing visions, including the face of a woman engulfed in flames that admonished him for setting the circus fire. "You are responsible," he claimed the vision had told him.

Segee admitted to setting the fire in Hartford, but he also said he did not remember doing it. He claimed that before the show, he'd been downtown on a date. When the girl rejected his advances, he went back to the circus grounds to take a nap. "I laid down and went to sleep and then there was the strike of the match again and the red man came," he related. "[I saw] a small flame and then it turned into this red man again and then the red man became a red horse and then I remembered somebody shaking me and when I came to I was standing on my feet with my clothing and shoes and stockings on and I ran in and tried to help with the people."

Throughout his interviews with Ohio authorities, Segee appeared remorseful, almost tearful. He claimed he was plagued by the visions that told him he had set the fires and was the cause of the victims' pain. He maintained throughout questioning that he did not remember setting the fire, but he felt his visions and mental anguish meant that surely he must be to blame. It appeared that Segee had difficulty distinguishing between his bad dreams and reality.

Was Segee guilty? He was known to set fires as a child and was about to be convicted for the Circleville fire. He had been at the scene of the crime. He had even confessed to setting the Hartford fire. However, the fact remained that no one had seen Segee set the circus fire. He himself said he did not remember doing it, and his unstable mental state made his admission of guilt dubious.

And then, on November 17, 1950, Segee recanted his confession.

Around this time, police in Scituate, Massachusetts, were eyeing Segee as a murder suspect. Two police sergeants were sent to interview him in prison to find out if they could connect him with the murder. They questioned him about his activities prior to the Hartford circus fire. During the course of the interview, Segee told the officers that he was not to blame for any of the fires he was accused of setting. He had never set a fire in his life, he said. Segee claimed that the accusations against him were based on his vivid dreams and imagination, rather than what he'd actually told investigators in Columbus. Segee now said he had not been on a date or returned to the grounds to take a nap before the fire started as he had previously stated. Instead he said that on the day of the circus fire, he and a friend had been downtown watching a movie. When Segee and his friend returned, the tent had already burned to the ground. He said they were questioned by officers and released. Segee was firm. He did not do it.

After Segee completed his prison sentence for the fire in Circleville, he was evaluated by another psychiatrist. The doctor diagnosed him as a paranoid schizophrenic and committed him to the Lima State Hospital for the Criminally Insane in Ohio.

Commissioner Hickey never got to interview his suspect, but the Ohio detectives hadn't cracked the case, either. The cause of the Hartford circus fire remained "accidental" for the next four decades—the prevailing theory: a carelessly discarded cigarette.

## – 1980s –

Lieutenant Rick Davey, an arson investigator for the Hartford fire department, had ferreted out the causes of thousands of fires during his career. He once boasted that every arson case he'd ever sent to court ended in a conviction. Though easygoing and soft spoken, he also had the determination of a salmon swimming upstream. People who have met him have called him tenacious and driven. If anyone could resolve the decades-old Hartford circus fire case, it was Davey.

Like most people who grew up in Hartford, Davey knew the story of the circus fire. But unlike those who casually read the news stories that reappeared on the anniversary every year, Davey had specialized knowledge. The idea that a carelessly tossed cigarette could have started the circus fire just didn't make sense to him. He wondered about factors such as the speed and temperature at which a cigarette burns, how much humidity was in the air that day, and whether a cigarette or even a used match dropped on dry grass really could catch fire.

Determining the true cause of the Hartford circus fire became a hobby for Lieutenant Davey. For nine years he studied the case in his spare time, spending countless hours at the archives of the Connecticut State Library, where boxes of materials related to the circus fire are housed. He collected evidence: photographs of the charred remains of the big top, weather records, and witness statements.

Davey dug through the reports from the state fire marshal and the mayor's special Board of Inquiry, and he reviewed the opinion of Thomas Brophy, the fire investigation expert from New York. The documents all discussed the possibility of the fire having been started by a carelessly tossed cigarette or used match. Commissioner Hickey's final report stated the fire started on the ground. Yet clearly it had started higher up on the tent wall, based on the hundreds of witness statements and supporting forensics. Davey felt that Hickey's report was wrong. There was no evidence that a cigarette had started the fire. In fact, Davey thought it very unlikely.

Davey wrote a report containing all the information he'd discovered and presented it to investigators at the Hartford fire marshal's office. Eventually the case was turned over to the Connecticut forensics laboratory. There the criminalists performed experiments, analyzed the data, and found the following:

- It was too humid on July 6, 1944, for a cigarette to start a fire.
- The grass around the big top had been cut just three days before; the trimmings would not have been dry enough to catch fire from a cigarette.
- The charring patterns on the bleacher seats where the fire started indicated that the fire was burning from the top, not from below on the grass.
- The grass under the bleachers was not burned.

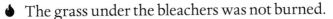

Their conclusions showed that a carelessly tossed cigarette did not start the Hartford circus fire.

Then how did it happen? Davey had another theory. He believed the fire was an act of arson—and he believed that Robert Segee, despite taking back his confession, had done it.

During his investigation, Davey had read the 1950 interviews with Robert Segee and the Ohio State Police reports that detailed Segee's confession. Unfortunately, Segee's mental instability made him an unreliable suspect, and there was no physical evidence that he had set the fire. When Segee recanted his confession, he claimed that he had been "harassed" into saying what the psychiatrist wanted to hear. But Davey knew the signs of an arsonist. He thought there was a good chance Segee was the one who had set the fire.

## – 1991 –

When Davey presented his report, Hartford police reopened the case and assigned Sergeant James Butterworth and Detective Bill Lewis to examine Segee as a suspect. Now 61 years old, Segee still denied setting the fire and told police and reporters to leave him alone. "The confession is not true," he told the *Hartford Courant* in 1991. "I really can't talk about this." Segee was unhappy that his name was being dredged up again as a suspect. "It's been very bad on me, and it was unjustified."

Butterworth and Lewis examined the suspect files for Robert Segee and read through the interviews from the investigation and Segee's mental evaluation in 1950. Lewis learned that the movie Segee claimed to have been watching downtown, *The Four Feathers*, was not playing at the time. Was Segee lying about his whereabouts at the start of the fire? His mental state may have been questionable, but Segee was definitely a strong suspect.

In March 1993, Butterworth and Lewis interviewed Segee at his home in Columbus, Ohio. Segee's daughter Carla was also there, supporting her father during the taped interview.

On the recording, the tone of the interview is friendly. The detectives assure Segee they have no evidence linking him to the Hartford fire and that they are merely there to find out the truth. Segee claims to want to tell the truth and to clear his name once and for all. At times during the interview he appears to plead with the detectives to believe him and says they're his "only chance."

Lewis and Butterworth ask questions about Segee's role in the circus and try to establish his whereabouts before, during, and after the fire. Segee tells the detectives that he worked for the lights department, where he was in charge of the big spotlight. On the afternoon of July 6 someone else took his place so he could go downtown to the movies. Unlike his statements in

1950, Segee now says he attended the movies alone and was not on a date or with a friend.

After the movie, Segee says, he got on the city bus, where he heard about the fire. When he got off at the circus grounds, the big top had already collapsed. Detective Lewis shows Segee a newspaper article from the days after the fire stating that Segee had been burned during the circus fire. But how could that be, if Segee was at the movies? Segee does not address this contradiction in the interview.

Segee tells Lewis and Butterworth it was at least a week after the fire before he was able to leave Hartford. "We was scrutinized pretty closely by the police department and things like that because of the fire," he tells them. According to Segee, the police questioned him, but only about where he was at the time of the fire, to which Segee responded he was downtown at the movies. Though the state archives have several thick folders of statements from circus employees, witnesses, police officers, and detectives, there does not seem to be a written statement from Robert Segee. In fact, there is no record of the police ever questioning Segee in the aftermath of the fire.

As the interview goes on, Segee's credibility becomes increasingly weak. When asked about his conviction in setting the fire in Circleville, Segee says he did not do it. He blames the politicians in Ohio for railroading him in order to get elected. "They wanted to clean the Goddamn book. So I was the perfect patsy." He goes on to blame Ringling Bros. for setting the fire in Hartford in order to collect the insurance money. Segee's tone makes it clear that he felt like everyone was out to get him.

Detective Lewis asks Segee about his visions and the pictures he drew while he was at the psychiatric hospital. Segee states several explanations: he did not draw them; they were falsified; if he did draw them, they actually reflect a vision of a battle in the late 1700s when Europeans set fire to the open plains after a fight with the Native Americans. The detectives ask about the "the red man" who Segee had said in his 1950 confession had told him to set the fire. "That don't mean nothing," Segee asserts on the recording. "They [the psychiatrists] made me do it. . . . Like I told ya, they messed with my brains."

And here is where the detectives probably realized they would never be able to pin the fire on Segee. Carla is heard on the recording: "You see, gentlemen, my father is Native American, and within the Native American community . . . as a holy man, as a shaman, yes, he has visions, but, a lot of times visions can be induced by talking to, in certain ways, where you would think you have seen this, or you have experienced this, but it actually did not come to pass."

Near the end of the interview, Segee seems tired and quieter than he'd been at the beginning. He again pleads with the detectives to believe him. He insists he is telling the truth about not setting any of the fires. The detectives maintain their even-handed tone throughout the interview, but they must have known they would not be returning to Hartford with any answers.

Butterworth: "I think the final question to ask, to nail this down is, did you start the Hartford circus fire?"

Segee: "No, sir. No, sir, I did not. I wasn't, I wasn't even on the grounds."

In the end, the Hartford police detectives were unable to make a case for arson. "With as many people that were there, no one saw anyone start this fire," Detective Lewis said following the interview with Segee. "Could it have been an arson fire? Our finding is undetermined. I have no evidence that it was an arson fire."

On June 30, 1993, the reexamination of Robert Segee in the case of the Hartford circus fire was closed. On August 10, because of Lieutenant Davey's research, the cause of the fire was officially changed from "Accidental" to "Undetermined." Though investigators all agreed that a carelessly tossed cigarette was not the cause of the fire, they still did not have any proof of arson.

Robert Segee died in August 1997. The cause of the Hartford circus fire, one of the most horrific disasters in New England's history, remains a mystery.

# 9

# A NAME FOR LITTLE MISS 1565

*"The eight-year-old who was partial to hair ribbons, cats and dresses has been known worldwide as Little Miss 1565. . . . Her name was Eleanor Cook."*

—Hartford Courant, *March 9, 1991*

Detectives Edward Lowe and Thomas Barber stood over the grave of Little Miss 1565, flowers dangling from their hands. The year was 1956. Twelve years had passed since the fire, and the identity of the little girl was still a mystery. Years before, the detectives had made a statement in the *Hartford Courant*, asking the community for help.

Somebody, somewhere must have cared enough for that little girl to take her to see the circus. In her own neighborhood, there must have been playmates, milkmen, grocery clerks, mailmen, and adults who noticed that some little girl was missing from their everyday lives. It just doesn't seem possible that a child like that little one could disappear from her own small world without somebody noticing that she had gone and never come back.

In all this time, they'd gotten few leads. Her morgue photo had circulated in newspapers across the county. In 1948, a woman from Michigan saw the photo and was certain Little Miss 1565 was her granddaughter whom she hadn't seen in four years. She informed the police, and the *Detroit Times* announced that Little Miss 1565 had been identified. However, soon after, the missing granddaughter and her mother called to say they were alive and well.

Someone suggested she was possibly a girl named Barbara Bluett from Hartford, and a friend of Detective Lowe said he thought Little Miss 1565 was his niece, Judith Berman. These turned out to be dead ends too.

Meanwhile, Donald Cook had grown up. He had never forgotten about his sister, Eleanor, who was lost in the circus fire. His mother kept up the hope that one day her daughter would appear at the door, but Donald knew she was never coming home. In fact, he had a theory. He believed that Little Miss 1565 was his sister.

In 1955, Donald was now 20 years old. He went to the Connecticut State Police and told them what he thought. But the case had been closed, and he got nowhere. Then, in a stroke of coincidence, he spoke about his family's tragedy with a coworker, Anna DeMatteo. She was struck by the sadness of his story and by his theory about Little Miss 1565. To her, it seemed believable. A year later, DeMatteo became a police officer in Connecticut, and she decided to look into Donald's story further. Unfortunately, after bringing the matter to her supervisors, she was unable to get them to reopen the case. The following letter to Officer DeMatteo shows a clear misunderstanding that must have been frustrating for her and for Donald.

Your report was reviewed by Chief Michael J. Godfrey, who recalls the persons involved in your report, and he personally talked with Mrs. Cook at the time of the fire.

The young man Donald, who gave you this information, must be misinformed because Mrs. Cook did lose a child in the Hartford circus fire, but it was a boy instead of a girl. Identification was made.

This matter can now be considered closed.

The officer is obviously referring to Donald's brother Edward, and makes no mention of Eleanor.

DeMatteo and Donald had hit a roadblock, but they didn't give up. In 1963, they tried again to connect Little Miss 1565 with Eleanor. In a long interview, Donald told DeMatteo everything he knew about the day of the fire and the attempts to find his sister during the aftermath. He explained that his family never discussed the tragedy because it was too painful. Eleanor was "the apple of their eye."

DeMatteo knew that Emily Gill said Little Miss 1565 was *not* Eleanor because she believed Eleanor had eight permanent upper teeth. Because permanent teeth generally grow on the top and bottom of the mouth in sets, having eight upper teeth would probably mean there are also eight lower teeth. If Emily were right, Eleanor would have had a total of 16 permanent teeth. Donald believed this could not have been true. Most children Eleanor's age have four permanent incisors (the top and bottom front teeth) as well as four permanent molars. Eleanor was too young to have had as many as 16 permanent teeth.

In the course of the interview, DeMatteo brought out a picture of Little Miss 1565. Donald had never seen the morgue photographs before. Now he took a long look. This little girl looked similar to his sister, he thought. Her teeth looked different than Eleanor's, but they had been damaged when the body was trampled during the fire. He thought the hair looked similar. The face looked the same, but Eleanor's "cheeks seemed rounder" in life. DeMatteo wrote in her notebook that Donald appeared shaken at viewing the photos of Little Miss 1565. Was it possible that he was looking at a photo of his long-lost sister?

*Let's talk to Aunt Marion*, Donald suggested. She'd raised the children for several years. Besides his mother, Marion knew the children best. Donald didn't want to show the photos to his mother yet because he wasn't absolutely sure his theory was true; he didn't want to cause her any more pain.

According to Donald, Aunt Marion had a sharp tongue. She seemed to be all business, the opposite of emotional Aunt Emily. When she met with Officer DeMatteo, she confirmed that the girl she'd seen at the armory back on July 6, 1944, was definitely not Eleanor. Her hair length had been wrong. The little girl had all but two baby teeth. Eleanor had eight permanent teeth, four upper and four lower. Marion clearly recalled that the little girl at the armory "had on a white dress, hardly touched by the fire at all." Eleanor did not own a dress like the one on the body. She believed Eleanor had been wearing a red playsuit on the day of the fire.

Officer DeMatteo spread the morgue photos of Little Miss 1565 on the table. There was silence, and Marion's eyes filled with tears. Marion thought the hair, the forehead, the shape of the eyebrows, the distance between the eyes, all looked like Eleanor. "This isn't the same little girl that I saw [at the armory]," she told DeMatteo. *Why wasn't I shown this little girl? Where was she when we were looking for Eleanor?* It seemed like Donald had been right all these years. Little Miss 1565 was his sister.

But Marion didn't want to make a quick decision. She met with another of Eleanor's aunts, Dorothy, and they looked at the photos together. At first, Dorothy thought the little girl resembled Eleanor. Then she changed her mind.

Marion too, despite her initial reaction, decided it must not be Eleanor after all. Only Donald still thought it was his sister, but he was concerned about the confusion regarding the number of permanent teeth. No one wanted to upset Mildred, so Marion and Dorothy decided to stand by their original decision: Little Miss 1565 was not Eleanor. Officer DeMatteo's investigation was over.

But that was not the last time Little Miss 1565 would be connected with Eleanor Cook. In 1991, Lieutenant Rick Davey, the same investigator who believed Robert Segee had set the fire, made an announcement that finally gave the people of Hartford a name for the unidentified little girl.

Davey's interest in the Hartford circus fire had begun in the 1980s. He'd given a talk about the fire at a junior high school and discovered the students knew more than he did about the subject. He promised to return when he knew more.

Davey began his research by looking through old editions of the *Hartford Courant* and moved on to the extensive archives at the Connecticut State Library. The more he found out about the mystery of Little Miss 1565, the more it haunted him. Davey asked the same questions others had for years: Who was this little girl? Why had no one claimed her? He was determined to figure out her identity.

It was Emily Gill's letter to Commissioner Hickey that led Davey to suspect that Little Miss 1565 was Eleanor Cook, though Emily had rejected this possibility. He compared the list of the unidentified bodies with the list of missing persons. Two little girls had never been found: Judy Norris and Eleanor Cook. Among the unidentified bodies there were two little girls, 1503 and

Little Miss 1565. It stood to reason, Davey thought, that Eleanor Cook was one and Judy Norris was the other.

The paper trail had led Davey to connect 1565 with Eleanor Cook. It was now up to him to address the road blocks that had come up in past investigations. There was little direct forensic evidence to go on, however, and Davey would have to rely heavily on the memory of Donald Cook to answer the questions others had raised. But Davey was persistent. He would make his case.

First, the body of Little Miss 1565 was dressed in a flowered white dress and brown shoes. Marion Parsons claimed that Eleanor did not own clothes like these. According to Davey, Donald told him that Mildred had given the children new clothes during their visit, and they'd been wearing them on the day of the fire.

And what about the difference in height between 1565 and Eleanor? In 1944, Eleanor's family had said that she was tall for her age, and Little Miss 1565 was only 46 inches tall. That would probably make her the shortest girl in her class. In a conflicting story, Davey claims that Donald had told him Eleanor had a disease called rickets, which would have stunted her growth.

The most useful piece of information Davey located in his search through the archives was the analysis of a hair sample. On July 15, 1944, hair samples from Eleanor were compared to hairs from the body of Little

Miss 1565 under a microscope. According to the doctor who compared the samples, "It may be concluded from this examination only that both specimens may have been derived from the same scalp. Absolute identification is, of course, impossible." What later happened to the hair samples themselves is unknown.

Davey compared morgue photographs of 1565 with a photo of Eleanor Cook. He analyzed the distance between the nose and the upper lip in each photo and found the measurements to be the same. He compared their earlobes (a method used by law enforcement before fingerprinting, though now rarely if ever used) and saw they were also similar. When he looked at the photos of Little Miss 1565, he thought about what fire and extreme heat can do to a body. It shrinks the ears and makes the nose look stubby. If 1565's ears and nose had not been altered by the fire, Davey thought, she would look more like Eleanor. Little Miss 1565's hair was mussed and her forehead bulged from being trampled. According to Davey, "Those changes in her appearance would have made it difficult, if not impossible, for her family to recognize the child they knew in life."

The number one problem in identifying Little Miss 1565 concerned her teeth. Davey looked at the dental chart for 1565. A copy of it was attached to her death certificate in the state library archives. According to the chart, 1565 had only two permanent teeth, incisors on the bottom. However, most eight-year-olds have between 6 and 10 permanent teeth, and Marion Parsons had said Eleanor had 8 permanent teeth. Davey claims the dentist who created the chart was wrong and that 1565 did have eight permanent teeth, making it more likely that 1565 was indeed Eleanor. However, there is no documented forensic evidence to support this claim. At the time of the fire, the family was unable to get Eleanor's dental records to compare with 1565 because the dentist had been on vacation. When the dentist returned, Little Miss 1565 had been buried, and the Cooks had already held a funeral for Eleanor. The family didn't pursue it further. Nearly 50 years later, there was no way to make a definitive comparison. According to Davey, the examiner's chart "seemed rather cursory in its assessments, so [he] did not consider it conclusive."

Donald had believed for years that Little Miss 1565 was his sister, and Lieutenant Davey was ready to support his claim. In 1991, Davey finalized his conclusions. Donald signed an official document affirming his belief that Little Miss 1565 was his sister Eleanor. Soon after, Davey received a report from Dr. Wayne Carver at the Connecticut medical examiner's office. After reviewing Davey's research, Dr. Carver issued a new death

Dental chart for unidentified victim 1565. The letter P written on the diagram indicates the two permanent teeth.

Eleanor Cook and her mother.

certificate, indicating that 1565 was indeed Eleanor Cook.

Elated to have his reward for many years of difficult research, Davey called Donald, and together they drove up to Massachusetts to speak with Mildred, who was now well into her 80s. When Davey told her that he had found her daughter at last, Mildred was happy. A long time had passed since she had lost her children. All her tears had been shed. Mildred did admit to Davey that even after all these years, she had still hoped Eleanor would "appear on the doorstep one day, without warning."

Months later, the body of Little Miss 1565 was removed from the plot in Northwood Cemetery near Hartford and brought to rest beside Edward Cook in Southampton, Massachusetts. The people of Hartford showed they would never forget the little girl they had looked after for so long. The original marker in Northwood was reinscribed:

RESTED IN PEACE HERE 47 YEARS AS
"LITTLE MISS"
1565
ON MARCH 8, 1991 SHE BECAME KNOWN AS
ELEANOR EMILY COOK,
AND IS NOW BURIED WITH HER FAMILY

The Hartford community has embraced Davey's conclusion that Little Miss 1565 is Eleanor Cook, but even today not everyone agrees with the outcome of his research. There are questions about his methods and about the lack of direct forensic evidence.

Are there enough similarities between 1565 and Eleanor to make a definitive conclusion? The lack of permanent teeth in 1565 is the most puzzling. It is unlikely that an eight-year-old girl would have only two permanent teeth. To explain this problem, Davey concluded that the dental chart was wrong and that 1565 did have eight permanent teeth. However, it is unlikely that that was the case. In Dr. Weissenborn's report to the coroner, it is clear that great care was taken to document all possible identifying details. According to the report, the dental chart; X-rays of the skull, teeth, and sinuses; and a picture of the body were sent to the coroner's office, the state police, and the city police of Hartford. It is true that we do not have Eleanor's dental records to compare to those of 1565; however, it seems likely that 1565's dental chart showing only two permanent teeth is correct. If Eleanor had more than two permanent teeth, she cannot be Little Miss 1565. Unfortunately, the X-rays done on 1565, including one showing the teeth, can no longer be found.

Other than the written analysis of the hair samples, which do not provide absolute proof, there is no official forensic evidence that links Little Miss 1565 to Eleanor. The paper trail shows investigators returning to Eleanor again and again, but that does not mean she is the unidentified girl.

Davey assumed that since there were two missing girls and two bodies of little girls, one of them must be Eleanor. In all, there were six unidentified bodies and six missing persons, but, as shown below, their descriptions do not match up.

| MISSING PERSONS | UNIDENTIFIED BODIES |
|---|---|
| Judy Norris, age 6 | 1503, female, 9 years old |
| Eleanor Cook, age 8 | 1565, female, 6 years old |
| Edith Budrick, age 38 | 4512, female, 35 years old |
| Raymond Erickson, age 6 | 1510, male, 11 years old |
| Grace Fifield, age 47 | 2109, female, 30 years old |
| Lucille Woodward, age 55 | 2200, male, 55 years old |

No one reported an adult male missing, but there's an unidentified male body. Three adult females were reported missing, but there are only two adult female bodies. When the medical examiner assessed the age and sex of the unidentified bodies, the remains—other than those of 1565—were almost unrecognizable.

Stewart O'Nan, a researcher and author on the subject of the circus fire, offers another striking possibility. Maybe *neither* of the unidentified girls is Eleanor. Twenty of the victims had been girls between the ages of six and nine years old. O'Nan says, "One mistake at the armory would throw the whole chain into chaos." Many of the bodies were difficult to identify, and families were understandably distressed. Is it possible that someone brought home the body of Eleanor and left their little girl behind? Could Eleanor have been buried in the plot of one of the other 19 little girls around her age?

Without forensic evidence, can we be sure that 1565 is indeed Eleanor Cook? In 1944, little was known about DNA; tests investigators use today to identify people had not yet been developed. Had DNA testing been available, it could have proven without a doubt whether 1565 was Eleanor by comparing her DNA with that of her brother. In 1991, when the body of Little Miss 1565 was moved to Southampton, no forensic evidence was collected. O'Nan claims that Donald had offered to give a DNA sample for confirmation, but no test was ever done.

Despite the many questions raised, Rick Davey and Don Massey, coauthors of a book describing Davey's investigations, are unwavering in their conclusion about Little Miss 1565. "There is no doubt in our minds who she is," Massey said to an audience in Hartford, Connecticut, in July 2010.

It is easy to see why so many people are facinated by the mystery of Little Miss 1565. Conflicting stories among Eleanor's family and decades of investigation seem to have led to more questions than answers. Is Little Miss 1565 Eleanor Cook? We may never know for sure.

We do know one thing: on a sunny July day, Eleanor Cook went to the circus with her family, but she, along with the 166 other victims of the Hartford circus fire, never came home. The community of Hartford mourned this tragedy as if each person who died was a member of the family. As the years go on, and the disaster has faded from the national newspapers, the people of Hartford still remember. Every July 6 the Hartford fire department holds a memorial service on the site where the big top tent once stood. Survivors and others gather each year so that the men, women, and children who were lost will live on in our memories.

# AUTHOR'S NOTE

I began researching and writing about the Hartford circus fire in 2005. That summer a memorial was unveiled on the exact spot on Barbour Street where the Ringling Bros. circus tent had stood on July 6, 1944. A bronze medallion surrounded by brick pavers and sandstone benches marks the location where the center pole had held up the enormous big top. Dogwood trees that line the perimeter of the field indicate the outer edges of the tent. Looking out at those trees, one can see just how huge the big top was.

I returned to the memorial site on July 6, 2014, to attend the 70th anniversary remembrance ceremony. It was a hot, cloudless day, though a breeze provided relief that those in 1944 never felt. The trees planted in 2005 had grown and now provided oases of shade. Survivors and their families gathered in folding chairs, some moving them under the shadow of the dogwoods. I recognized familiar faces in the crowd, people I had interviewed, including survivors Harry Lichtenbaum, Barbara Wallis Felgate, and Bob O'Connell. The

Hartford Circus Fire Memorial.

survivors are older; many are now gone. Noticeably absent was retired Lieutenant Rick Davey, who had moved to Florida. For many years, Davey had been the memorial's guardian and keeper. It was he who would get down on the ground and repaint the names and remembrances printed on the bricks whenever they began to fade.

At exactly 2:40 PM, memorial organizers rang a bell and then read the names of all 167 victims of the fire. After the last name was read, I heard the distant whistle of a train, and it felt as if the circus had come to town once more to pay its respects.

We had gathered to remember an event that changed so many lives, to provide comfort, and to commemorate the loss. That's the power of community, to universally share in the hurt when we lose someone we love. Yes, the Hartford circus fire was one of America's greatest disasters, but out of the ashes we find out just how resilient we can be. We survive, we remember, we love.

At the end of my research into the Hartford circus fire, questions still remain. Among them, did troubled 15-year-old Robert Segee set the fire? And is Eleanor Cook Little Miss 1565? Having questions helps us realize that history is not just a collection of facts, dates, and names. History is made up of the stories of people's lives. We ask questions because we want to know the truth, not only for ourselves, but for those who survive and also for the sake of others who've lost their lives in these kinds of tragedies. Even if our questions don't lead us to answers, they help us remember and honor our past.

In researching the Hartford circus fire, I consulted many sources, including books, documentaries, and newspaper and magazine articles about the fire. I conducted personal interviews, and I dug through the boxes and boxes of material on the circus fire collected by the outstanding librarians at the Connecticut State Library Archives. As my research progressed, it became clearer to me than ever that the word of one person may not hold the truth. In fact, the words of many people may still leave questions unanswered. I believe the best way to decide for yourself just how close you can get to the truth is to ask questions of as many people as possible. I hope that I have done justice to this effort.

# ACKNOWLEDGMENTS

An abundance of thanks to: Lisa Reardon and the folks at Chicago Review Press; Mike Skidgell, who provided an expert review of this book—any remaining mistakes of fact are mine; Stewart O'Nan, a source of information and encouragement right from the start; the spectacular librarians at the Connecticut State Library, the Hartford Public Library, and the Connecticut Historical Society; Susan Bloom, the first reader of my manuscript; Courtney (Bonner) Saldana, my first "research assistant"; the Gripers (Elaine Dimopoulos, Jane Kohuth, Kirsty McKay, Sonia Miller, and Jean Stehle Roy) for their tireless enthusiasm in reading my many, many drafts; SCBWI and James Cross Giblin for the Work-In-Progress grant that enabled me to discover the treasure trove at the Connecticut State Library archives; Lisa Paradis for going to the circus with me; and my parents and husband (and basically anyone in earshot) for listening to me ramble about my project. Thank you.

# NOTES

## CHAPTER ONE:
## THE CIRCUS COMES TO TOWN

*"Coming from Providence"*: Hartford Courant, July 5, 1944.

*"the real Fairyland . . . "*: Ringling Bros. and Barnum & Bailey Circus program, 1944 season.

*"they want to laugh . . . "*: Ringling Bros. and Barnum & Bailey Circus program, 1944 season.

*"Good Salary and Expenses . . . "*: Billboard, May 16, 1944.

## CHAPTER TWO:
## "THE GREATEST SHOW ON EARTH"

*"The last word in high wire thrillers"*: 1944 Ringling Bros. and Barnum & Bailey Circus program, 1944 season.

"*The air was stagnant . . .* ": Personal interview with Arthur S. Lassow, July 6, 2005.

"*I was awestruck . . .* ": *The Circus Fire,* Connecticut Public Television (CPTV), 2000.

**CHAPTER THREE: FIRE!**

"*We heard a roar, like the applause*": *Providence Journal,* July 7, 1944.

"*There's a fire over there*": Personal interview with Donalda (LaVoie) Matthews, July 6, 2005.

"*I was watching the lions . . .* ": Personal interview with Barbara Wallis Felgate, July 6, 2005.

"*I came right through the doorway*": Personal interview with Rose Norrie, July 6, 2005.

"*I grabbed the hand of my niece Judy . . .* ": Witness statement of Margaret D'Abatto.

"*[I] noticed a girl about five years old . . .* ": Letter from Donald Anderson to Governor Baldwin, October 2, 1944.

"*When the fire broke out . . .* ": Telephone interview with Eugene Badger, August 11, 2005.

"*My hand got torn out of my mother's . . .* ": *The Circus Fire,* CPTV, 2000.

"*My foot kind of slipped . . .* ": Personal interview with Donalda (LaVoie) Matthews, July 6, 2005.

*"Let my little boy through"*: Telephone interview with Phil Handler, July 15, 2014.

*"People couldn't get past . . . "*: *News Channel 8*, wtnh.com, July 6, 2005.

*"Some dirty son of a bitch tossed . . . "*: McAuliffe police statement, July 8, 1944.

## CHAPTER FOUR: "THE DAY THE CLOWNS CRIED"

*"Tumult and wild disorder"*: *Hartford Times*, July 6, 1944 (extra edition).

*"one woman, who was joined by a man . . . "*: *Hartford Courant*, July 7, 1944.

*"I went back to my car . . . "*: *Providence Journal*, July 7, 1944.

*"We saw a woman come running out . . . "*: Telephone interview with Eugene Badger, August 11, 2005.

*"The circus people were wonderful"*: *Hartford Courant*, July 7, 1944.

*"They were so calm . . . "*: *Hartford Times*, July 6, 1944.

*"The circus animals were comparatively quiet . . . "*: *Boston Globe*, July 7, 1944.

*"It was an ideal time for kids . . . "*: Telephone interview with Guy Cummings, August 16, 2010.

*"We were repairing a meter . . . "*: Weinstein police statement.

*"We can be intensely proud"*: The Hartford Circus Fire: An Audio Recollection, University of Hartford radio WWUH, July 7, 2005.

*"request for Type O blood . . . "*: The Hartford Circus Fire: An Audio Recollection, University of Hartford radio WWUH, July 7, 2005.

*"Telephone service throughout Greater Hartford . . ."*: Hartford Courant, July 7, 1944.

*"Mom, we're all right"*: Unpublished article by Harry Lichtenbaum.

*"hysteria will only add to the confusion"*: The Hartford Circus Fire: An Audio Recollection, University of Hartford radio WWUH, July 7, 2005.

## CHAPTER FIVE: MUNICIPAL HOSPITAL

*"We had two hands and did whatever we could"*: Hartford Courant, July 7, 1944 (morning edition).

*"Please all of you . . . "*: Hartford Courant, July 7, 1944.

*"People as a whole were well behaved"*: Hartford Courant, July 7, 1944.

*"a couple of pinkies"*: Telephone interview with Shirley Lawton, April 2, 2014.

*"I'll never forget the children . . . "*: Telephone interview with Kenneth Sinkwitz, July 10, 2005.

*"Those were the worst times"*: The Circus Fire, CPTV, 2000.

*"Remember the girl . . . "*: Smith personal notebook, Connecticut State Library Archives.

## CHAPTER SIX: "WHO KNOWS THIS CHILD?"

*"Into the big drill shed"*: *Hartford Times*, July 6, 1944 (extra edition).

*"some were so stricken . . . "*: *Boston Globe*, July 7, 1944.

*"please stay away from the armory . . . "*: *The Hartford Circus Fire: An Audio Recollection*, University of Hartford radio WWUH, July 7, 2005.

*"I was the one who found . . . "*: E-mail correspondence with Bob O'Connell, July 15, 2014.

*"So long as I know"*: *Boston Globe*, July 7, 1944.

*"I've been a cop for 25 years . . . "*: *Boston Globe*, July 7, 1944.

*"This was the one that she had looked at . . . "*: Freeman police report, July 8, 1944.

*"Neighborhood dentist in Southampton . . ."*: Dental chart of 1503, Connecticut State Library Archives.

*"Dear Mr. Hickey . . . "*: Letter from Emily Gill to Commissioner Hickey, July 20, 1944.

*"Who Knows This Child"*: *Hartford Times*, July 12, 1944.

## CHAPTER SEVEN: WHO WAS TO BLAME?

*"Seven officials and employees"*: *Hartford Courant*, January 12, 1945.

*"the armed forces had exclusive control . . . "*: Cohn Report, undated.

*"The report finds no legal responsibility . . . "*: *Hartford Times*, January 12, 1945.

## CHAPTER EIGHT: ACCIDENT OR ARSON?

*"An investigation of the cause"*: Report of Commissioner of State Police, January 11, 1945.

*"tossed or dropped a cigarette . . . "*: McAuliffe police statement, July 8, 1944.

*"That dirty son-of-a-b---- just threw a cigarette butt"*: Report of Commissioner of State Police, January 11, 1945.

*"a cigarette would have smoked . . . "*: Report of Commissioner of State Police, January 11, 1945.

*"Coroner: Supposing your chemical analysis . . . "*: Hickey statement, August 10, 1944.

*"At about the end of the animal [act] . . . "*: Pelton witness statement.

*"a patch of flame . . . "*: Fyler witness statement.

*"I sat . . . about two seats from the top . . ."*: Dewey witness statement.

*"Many patrons for the first time . . . "*: Report of Commissioner of State Police, January 11, 1945.

*"Upon the testimony before me . . . "*: Report of Commissioner of State Police, January 11, 1945.

*"It appeared throughout our investigation . . . "*: Letter from Lavin to Hickey, May 25, 1950.

*"was always very mean to Robert . . . "*: Robert Segee's confession, June 27, 1950.

*"You are responsible"*: Robert Segee's confession, June 27, 1950.

"*I laid down and went to sleep . . .* ": Robert Segee's confession, June 27, 1950.

"*The confession is not true*": Hartford Courant, March 13, 1991.

"*only chance*": Robert Segee interview by James Butterworth and Bill Lewis, March 16–17, 1993.

"*We was scrutinized . . .* ": Robert Segee interview, March 16–17, 1993.

"*They wanted to clean the Goddamn book . . .* ": Robert Segee interview, March 16–17, 1993.

"*That don't mean nothing*": Robert Segee interview, March 16–17, 1993.

"*You see, gentlemen . . .* ": Robert Segee interview, March 16–17, 1993.

"*I think the final question . . .* ": Robert Segee interview, March 16–17, 1993.

"*With as many people that were there . . .* ": The Circus Fire, CPTV, 2000.

## CHAPTER NINE:
## A NAME FOR LITTLE MISS 1565

"*The eight-year-old who was partial to hair ribbons*": Hartford Courant, March 9, 1991.

"*Somebody, somewhere must have cared . . .* ": Hartford Courant, July 7, 1945.

*"Your report was reviewed . . . "*: Letter to Anna DeMatteo from Connecticut State Police, April 23, 1956.

*"the apple of their eye"*: DeMatteo notebook, Connecticut State Library Archives.

*"cheeks seemed rounder"*: DeMatteo notebook , Connecticut State Library Archives.

*"had on a white dress . . . "*: DeMatteo notebook, Connecticut State Library Archives.

*"This isn't the same little girl . . . "*: DeMatteo notebook, Connecticut State Library Archives.

*"It may be concluded from this examination . . . "*: Notes from Department of State Police, July 15, 1944.

*"Those changes in her appearance . . . "*: Davey and Massey, *A Matter of Degree*, 238.

*"seemed rather cursory in its assessments . . . "*: *A Matter of Degree*, 236.

*"appear on the doorstep one day . . . "*: *A Matter of Degree*, 269.

*"One mistake at the armory . . . "*: O'Nan, *The Circus Fire*, 353.

*"There is no doubt . . . "*: Don Massey, presentation at Mark Twain Museum, July 6, 2010.

# BIBLIOGRAPHY

## FROM THE CONNECTICUT STATE ARCHIVES

### Legal Documents

*State v. Ringling Bros.–Barnum & Bailey Combined Shows, Inc. a Delaware Corporation, James A. Haley, George W. Smith, Leonard S. Aylesworth, Edward R. Versteeg, David W. Blanchfield, and William Caley. Superior Court.* Jan. session, 1945.

*State of CT v. Ringling Bros. and Barnum and Bailey Combined Shows Inc., et al. Motion for suspension of sentences and leave to withdraw pleas.* March 27, 1945.

### Official Reports

*Casualty Lists.* RG 161. Dept. of Public Safety, Division of State Police. Investigation Files. Box 1, Folders 14, 15.

*Casualty List.* Appendix II. Office of the Public Records Administrator and State Archives. Subject Guide to the Hartford Circus Fire, July 6, 1944. 2nd ed., Connecticut State Library, 2002.

*Coroner's Report. Memorandum to Coroner Healy: July 18, 1944.* RG 161. Dept. of Public Safety, Division of State Police. Investigation Files. Box 3, Folder 3.

*Criminal Files, Hartford Superior Court.* 13599-16671. 1937–1945. Box 24, File #16579.

*Hartford Board of Inquiry on the Circus Disaster.* Report of the Municipal Board of Inquiry. Includes Lease of Grounds, Performance License. Special Collection. TH9449.H3 A5 1944.

*Hartford County Coroner Records 1883–1979.* RG 161. Dept. of Public Safety, Division of State Police. Investigation Files. Box 16, Folder 3.

*Hartford Police Department, Office of the Chief, Official or Confidential Report,* July 3, 1944. RG 161. Dept. of Public Safety, Division of State Police. Investigation Files. Box 1, Folder 6.

*Record of Inquest Held on the Body of Miss Elaine B. Akerlind, and 167 Others Who Died as a Result of the Circus Disaster, July 6, 1944, at Hartford, Conn.* Report written by Frank E. Healy, Coroner for Hartford County. RG 161. Dept. of Public Safety, Division of State Police. Investigation Files. Box 3, Folder 3.

*Re-Examination Forensic Report 1993.* RG 161. Dept. of Public Safety, Division of State Police. Investigation Files. Box 1, Folders 1, 3.

*Report on Circus Disaster July 14, 1944. To Mr. Henry B. Mosle, Administrator From Ralph S. Goodsell, Protective Division.* RG 161. Dept. of Public Safety, Division of State Police. Investigation Files. Box 3, Folder 4.

*Report of Commissioner of State Police as State Fire Marshal to State's Attorney for Hartford County Concerning the Fire in Hartford on July 6, 1944 at the Ringling Bros.–Barnum & Bailey Combined Shows, Inc.,* January 11, 1945. ConnDoc F51r c.3.

*Report of Henry Cohn, Attorney for the State of Connecticut,* undated. RG 069. Manuscripts Collections. Box 1, Folder "Dr. Milton Fleisch."

*Report of Officer S.E. Freeman,* July 8, 1944. RG 161. Dept. of Public Safety, Division of State Police. Investigation Files. Box 3, Folder 8.

*Report of Investigators Paul Lavin and Paul Beckwith,* May 25, 1950. RG 161. Dept. of Public Safety, Division of State Police. Investigation Files. Box 7, Folder 1.

*Robert Segee's Confession and Statements from Dorothy Segee Thompson and Amy Josephine (Aspinall) Segee.* State of Ohio Department of Commerce, Division of State Fire Marshal, Arson Bureau. Investigation Report, Privileged and Confidential. Columbus, Ohio, June 27, 1950. RG 161. Dept. of Public Safety, Division of State Police. Investigation Files. Box 6, Folder 8.

*State Highway Patrol Report of Investigation, November 21, 1950.* RG 161. Dept. of Public Safety, Division of State Police. Investigation Files. Box 7, Folder 3.

*Suspect File for Robert Segee.* Includes psychological report from Lima State Hospital, Aug. 19, 1950. RG 161. Dept. of Public Safety, Division of State Police. Investigation Files. Box 6, Folder 7.

*War Council Reports. Notes on the Organization of the State E.M.S. of the War Council at the State Armory, Hartford, Connecticut, July 6–July 9, 1944 During Crisis of Hartford Fire.* RG 161. Dept. of Public Safety, Division of State Police. Investigation Files. Box 3, Folder 4.

*Weather Report.* RG 161. Dept. of Public Safety, Division of State Police. Investigation Files. Box 3, Folder 5.

### Personal Letters and Notes

*Edward Lowe Collection, Elliot Smith Collection,* RG 069:112, Manuscripts Collections, Box 1.

*Letter from Donald Anderson to Governor Baldwin,* October 2, 1944, RG 005, Records of the Governors, Box 451.

*Letter from Anna DeMatteo to Connecticut State Police,* April 18, 1956, RG 161. Dept. of Public Safety, Division of State Police. Investigation Files. Box 3, Folder 7.

*Letter to Anna DeMatteo from the Connecticut State Police,* April 23, 1956, RG 161. Dept. of Public Safety, Division of State Police. Investigation Files. Box 3, Folder 8.

*Letter from Emily Gill to Commissioner Hickey,* July 20, 1944, RG 161. Dept. of Public Safety, Division of State Police. Investigation Files. Box 3, Folder 6.

*Letter to Commissioner Hickey from Investigator Paul Lavin,* May 25, 1950, RG 161. Dept. of Public Safety, Division of State Police. Investigation Files. Box 7, Folder 3.

*Notebook of Anna DeMatteo,* RG 161. Dept. of Public Safety, Division of State Police. Investigation Files. Box 3, Folder 8.

*Notes from Department of State Police, July 15, 1944 about hair samples from Eleanor Cook and Unidentified body of small girl approx. 6 yrs. of age,* Lincoln Opper, M.D., Director of Clinical Laboratories, RG 161. Dept. of Public Safety, Division of State Police. Investigation Files. Box 3, Folder 6.

*Robert Segee's school records,* City of Portland, Maine. Police Department, June 8, 1950, RG 161. Dept. of Public Safety, Division of State Police. Investigation Files. Box 7, Folder 2.

## Photographs

*Armory photographs.* RG 161. Dept. of Public Safety, Division of State Police. Investigation Files. Box 4, Folder 8.

*Circus employee photographs.* RG 161. Dept. of Public Safety, Division of State Police. Investigation Files. Box 4, Folder 9.

*Circus grounds before and after the fire.* RG 161. Dept. of Public Safety, Division of State Police. Investigation Files. Box 1, Folder 5.

*General photographs.* RG 161. Dept. of Public Safety, Division of State Police. Investigation Files. Box 4, Folders 6, 7.

*Hospital photographs.* RG 161. Dept. of Public Safety, Division of State Police. Investigation Files. Box 4, Folder 10.

*Gladys Nelson Collection.* RG 069. Manuscripts Collections. Box 1, Folder "Nelson Collection."

*Robert Segee Artwork.* RG 161. Dept. of Public Safety, Division of State Police. Investigation Files. Box 7, Folder 7.

*Unidentified body, Little Miss 1565.* RG 161. Dept. of Public Safety, Division of State Police. Investigation Files. Box 3, Folder 9.

*Carl Wallis photographs.* RG 161. Dept. of Public Safety, Division of State Police. Investigation Files. Box 4, Folder 4.

## Ringling Bros. and Barnum & Bailey Circus Publicity Materials

*Ringling Bros. and Barnum & Bailey 1944 tour handbill.* RG 161. Dept. of Public Safety, Division of State Police. Investigation Files. Box 3, Folder 7.

*Ringling Bros. and Barnum & Bailey Circus program, 1944 season.* RG 161. Dept. of Public Safety, Division of State Police. Investigation Files. Box 1, Folder 4.

## Statements and Interviews

*Detective Statements.* RG 161. Dept. of Public Safety, Division of State Police. Investigation Files. Box 1, Folder 7.

*Hartford Police Statements.* RG 161. Dept. of Public Safety, Division of State Police. Investigation Files. Box 1, Folder 13.

*Direct examination of New York Fire Marshal Thomas B. Brophy, by Coroner Frank E. Healy.* RG 161. Dept. of Public Safety, Division of State Police. Investigation Files. Box 3, Folder 3.

*Robert Segee Interview by Sgt. James Butterworth and Detective Bill Lewis,* March 16–17, 1993. RG 161. Audio tapes and transcription. Dept. of Public Safety, Division of State Police. Investigation Files. Box 1, Folder 2.

*Statement of Commissioner E. J. Hickey, continued, given to coroner August 10, 1944.* RG 161. Dept. of Public Safety, Division of State Police. Investigation Files. Box 3, Folder 3.

*Statement of William H. Cronin, Department Clerk, concerning issuance of circus license for Ringling Bros.–Barnum & Bailey Combined Shows, Inc.* RG 161. Dept. of Public Safety, Division of State Police. Investigation Files. Box 1, Folder 5.

*Telegraph from Commissioner Hickey, State Fire Marshal to Harry Callan, State Fire Marshal, Columbus, Ohio.* RG 161. Dept. of Public Safety, Division of State Police. Investigation Files. Box 7, Folder 1.

*Telephone conversations between Commissioner Hickey and Harry Callan.* RG 161. Dept. of Public Safety, Division of State Police. Investigation Files. Box 7, Folders 1, 3.

*Witness statements.* RG 161. Dept. of Public Safety, Division of State Police. Investigation Files. Box 3, Folders 1, 2.

## NEWSPAPER AND MAGAZINE ARTICLES

*Boston Globe*: July 6, 1944 (evening edition); July 7, 1944 (morning and evening editions); July 8, 1944 (morning and evening editions).

Bradbury, Joseph T., "The Season of 1944 Ringling Bros. and Barnum & Bailey Circus," *The White Tops Magazine*, May–June 1981, vol. 45, no. 3.

*Hartford Courant*: July 5, 1944; July 7, 1944 (morning edition); January 12, 1945; January 20, 1945; February 1, 1945; February 22, 1945; February 23, 1945; July 7, 1945; Aug 16, 1945; July 4, 1950; March 9, 1991; March 13, 1991; March 17, 1991; June 22, 1991; June 23, 1991; July 6, 1991; July 5, 2005; July 7, 2005.

*Hartford Times*: July 6, 1944 (extra edition); July 12, 1944; November 17, 1944; November 21, 1944; December 1, 1944; January 9, 1945; January 12, 1945; January 20, 1945; February 1, 1945; February 21, 1945; February 23, 1945; April 21, 1945; June 8, 1945; July 17, 1945; May 22, 1950; August 27, 1952; July 7, 1956.

*Providence Journal*: July 2, 1944; July 3, 1944; July 7, 1944; July 8, 1944; July 9, 1944.

*News Channel 8*: July 6, 2005 (article found online at www.wtnh.com).

*New York Times*, July 7, 1944; July 8, 1944.

*Newsweek*, July 17, 1944.

*Life Magazine*, July 17, 1944; July 17, 1950.

*Time Magazine*, July 17, 1944.

Tuohy, Lynne, "Eternal Flame," *Northeast Magazine*, supplement to the Sunday *Hartford Courant*, July 7, 1991.

## BOOKS

Cohn, Henry S. and David Bollier. *The Great Hartford Circus Fire*. New Haven, CT: Yale University Press, 1991.

Massey, Don and Rick Davey. *A Matter of Degree*. Simsbury, CT: Willow Brook Press, 2001.

O'Nan, Stewart. *The Circus Fire*. New York: Anchor Books, 2000.

Skidgell, Michael. *The Hartford Circus Fire*. Charleston, SC: The History Press, 2014.


## RADIO, TELEVISION, AND THEATER

*The Circus Fire*. Connecticut Public Television (CPTV), 2000.

*Front Street*, by playwright Anne Pié. Presented by the Little Theater of Manchester. Manchester, Connecticut, August 20, 2005.

*The Hartford Circus Fire: An Audio Recollection*. Hosted by Brandon Kampe. Presented by University of Hartford radio station WWUH (includes recordings of radio news broadcasts from 1944), recorded July 13, 2005.

*Wrath of God: Fire Under the Big Top*. The History Channel, 2000.

## PERSONAL INTERVIEWS WITH THE AUTHOR

Eugene Badger
Mauro Balboni
Kirsten Freeburg Cassarino
Dick Connolly
Guy Cummings
Jeff Cummings
Jane Diana
Anna DiMartino
Lorena Dutelle
Barbara Wallis Felgate
Linnea Freeburg
Phil Handler
Arthur S. Lassow
Shirley Lawton
Harry Lichtenbaum
Donalda (LaVoie) Matthews
Rose Norrie
Bob O'Connell
Barbara Schweitzer
Kenneth Sinkwitz
Lillian Tetreault
Calvin Vinick

# IMAGE CREDITS

Page 9: Courtesy of the Connecticut State Library, State Police Investigation Files, RG 161

Pages 10–11: Courtesy of Dan McGinnis Sr.

Page 15: Courtesy of the Connecticut State Library, State Police Investigation Files, RG 161.

Page 17: Courtesy of the Connecticut State Library, State Police Investigation Files, RG 161

Page 19: James Spence

Page 26: Courtesy of the Connecticut Historical Society

Page 28: Courtesy of the Connecticut Historical Society

Pages 32–33: Courtesy of the Connecticut State Library, Gladys Nelson Collection, RG 069

Pages 38–39: Courtesy of the Connecticut State Library, State Police Investigation Files, RG 161

Page 43: Photo by Ralph Emerson Sr., courtesy of Michael Skidgell

Page 44: Courtesy of the Connecticut State Library, State Police Investigation Files, RG 161

Page 46: Courtesy of the Connecticut State Library, State Police Investigation Files, RG 161

Pages 48–49: Courtesy of the Hartford History Center, Hartford Public Libarary

Page 53: Courtesy of the Connecticut State Library, State Police Investigation Files, RG 161

Page 56: Courtesy of the Connecticut State Library, State Police Investigation Files, RG 161

Page 58: Courtesy of the Connecticut State Library, State Police Investigation Files, RG 161

Page 61: ACME photo, courtesy of Michael Skidgell

Page 65: AP Wirephoto, courtesy of Michael Skidgell

Page 69: Courtesy of the Connecticut State Library, State Police Investigation Files, RG 161

Pages 82–83: Courtesy of the Hartford History Center, Hartford Public Library

Page 87: Courtesy of the Connecticut State Library, State Police Investigation Files, RG 161

Page 93: Photo by Wesley Mason, courtesy of the Connecticut State Library, State Police Investigation Files, RG 161

Page 95: Photo by Spencer Torell, courtesy of the Connecticut Historical Society

Page 97: Courtesy of the Connecticut State Library, State Police Investigation Files, RG 161

Page 98: Courtesy of the Connecticut State Library, State Police Investigation Files, RG 161

Page 123: Courtesy of the Connecticut State Library, State Police Investigation Files, RG 161

Page 124: Courtesy of the Connecticut State Library, State Police Investigation Files, RG 161

Page 132: Photo by the author

# INDEX

Page numbers in **bold** denote illustrations.

## A

animal chutes, 2, 21–22, 30–31, 45, 59, 83, **84–85**, 92
animal trainers, 7, 11, 20–21, 31, 42
arson, 93–113
Aylesworth, Leonard, 88, **89**

## B

Badger, Eugene, 16–18, 27, 29, 41, 156

Barber, Thomas, 88, 115
bears, 14, 20
Beckwith, Paul, 88, 101
Berman, Judith, 116
big top tent **10**
    burning of, **26, 32, 33**
    diagram of, **19**
    flammability of, 2, 37, 83, 86, 94
    remains of, **38, 39, 46**
    waterproofing of, 2, 83
Blanchfield, David, **89**, 89
blood donors, 17, 50, 56
Bluett, Barbara, 116
*Boston Globe*, 42, 66, 69

Boston nightclub fire (1942), 57

Boy Scouts, 51

Brickley, William J., 56

Brophy, Thomas, 94–95, 106

Brown School, 52, **53**, 62, 69–70

Brown, Ella, 52

Butterworth, James, 108–110, 112

## C

Caley, William, 89–90

Carver, Wayne, 124

cigarettes, *See* smoking

circus fires, 7–8, 14, 42, 82, 86, 100

Cleveland Ringling Bros. fire (1942), 14, 42, 86

clowns, 4, 8, 18, 42

Cohn, Henry, 83

Connecticut
governor of, 27, 50
lawyers for, 83

Connecticut medical examiner, 124

Connecticut State Armory, 54, 65–67, **67**, 69–70, 72–73, 75, 77, 130

Connecticut State Library, 106, 121, 123, 136

Connecticut state police, 74, 117
*See also* Hickey, Edward

Connecticut War Council, 52, 66

Connors, Marie Ann, 60

Cook, Donald, 8, **9**, 25, 27, 40, 64, 77, 116–120, 122, 124, 127

Cook, Edward, 8, **9**, 27, 29–30, 62, 64, 73, 77, 118
grave of, 127

Cook, Eleanor, 8, **9**, 27, 30, 76, 115, 118, 120–124, **126**, 127–131
dental records, 73–75, 118, 124, 128
disappearance of, 64, 70–74, 77, 116
*See also* "Little Miss 1565"

Cook, Mildred, 8, 10, 18, 25, 27, 29–30, 62, 64, 73–74, 77, 120, 122, 126–127

coroner, 78, 88, 96, 128

Cummings, Guy and Jeff, 45, 156

Curlee, David, 31

Curlee, William, 31, 34

**D**

Davey, Rick, 105–108, 112, 121–124, 127–129, 131, 135

DeMatteo, Anna, 117–120

dental records, 70–75, 118–119, 123–125, 128

*Detroit Times*, 116

Dewey, Joseph, 97

DNA, 130, 131

Dutelle, Lorena, 29, 156

**E**

elephants, 7, 11, 14–15, 42

emergency vehicles, 47, 91

**F**

Felgate, Barbara Wallis, 24, 134, 156

fire victims, 2, 47, 51, 54–55, 57

   bodies of, 54, 65–66, 78

   claims of, 90

   long–term effects of fire, 91

   memorial to, 135

firefighters, 47, 91

   *See also* Hartford fire department

Flying Wallendas, *See* Wallenda family

Freeman, Sam, 74–76

Fyler, Helen, 97

**G**

Gale, Donald, 16, 45, 62

Gill, Emily (Parsons), 62, 64, 70, 76, 118, 121

giraffes, 14–15

Godfrey, Michael J., 117

Goodman, Leo, **46**

gorillas, 3–4, 14–16

Gwinnell, Kenneth, 95–96, 98

## H

Haley, James, 88, **89**

Hallissey, Charles, 87

Handler, Morris, 31

Handler, Phil, 31, 156

Hartford
  disaster preparedness, 47
  mayor of, 58, 90
  Northwood Cemetery, 78, 127
  responsibility for fire, 86

Hartford Board of Inquiry, 82, 106

Hartford Circus Fire Memorial, 133, **134**

*Hartford Courant*, 3, 40–41, 51, 55, 57, 66, 81, 108, 115, 121

Hartford fire department, 86, 87, 105
  memorial services, 131
  new regulations, 91

Hartford Hospital, 53, 57, 62, 74

Hartford police department, 34, 47, **48**, 51–52, 66, 68–69, 112

*Hartford Times*, 37, 42, 51, 65, 78

Hathaway, Helen, 42

Hayes, Charles, 87

Healy, Frank E., 96

Hickey, Edward, 74, 76, 83, 93, 96, 100–101, 105, 121
  report of, 94, 98, 106–107

Higley, Bernard, 102

hippotamuses, 14

Hopkins, Robert Jr., **58**

## K

Kelly, Emmett, 4–5, 42, **43**

Kovar, May, 20–21, 31

## L

LaMonda, Detective, 101

Lassow, Arthur S., 13, 156

Lavin, Paul, 101

LaVoie, Donalda, 23, 30, 156

Lawton, Shirley, 58–59, 156

LeVasseur, Jerry, 59–60, 62

Lewis, Bill, 108–112

Lichtenbaum, Harry, 51, 134, 156lions, 14, 20, 24

"Little Miss 1565," 79, 115–124, 126–131

    dental chart, 125

    graves of, 78, 127

    *See also* Cook, Eleanor

Lowe, Edward, 88, 115–116

**M**

McAuliffe, Daniel, 34, 94, 98

MacRae, Donald, **58**

Massey, Don, 131

morgue, 54, 65

    numbers, 75, 79

Mortensen, William H., 58, 90

Municipal Hospital, 53, 55–64, **63**, 74, 76

Murphy, Patty, 62, **63**

**N**

National Guard, 50, 65

Norrie family, 25, 156

Norris, Judy, 121–122, 129

North, John Ringling, 83

nurses, **48**, 55–57, 59–61, 68, 70

    volunteer, 50, 56, 58

**O**

O'Connell, Doris Jean, 68

O'Connell, E. J., 68

O'Nan, Stewart, 130

**P**

Parsons, Marion, 8, 64, 72–73, 76–77, 119–120, 122, 124

Parsons, Ted, 8, 62, 72, 76

Pastizzo, Anthony, 20

Pelton, Jane, 96

penicillin, 56

police, *See* Connecticut state police; Hartford police department

*Providence Journal*, 23, 40

## R

radio, 50, 52, 66
railroads, 5
Red Cross, 17, 50
Ringling Bros. & Barnum
    and Bailey Circus, 3–6,
    8–11, 13, 14–22
        responsibility for fire,
            46–47, 81–92, 98–99,
            111
        victim relief, 51
        workers, 41, **89**, 98
Rubenthaler, Barbara, 34

## S

Segee, Carla, 109, 111–112
Segee, Josephine, 101
Segee, Robert, 6, 11, 45, 99,
    **100**, 101–105, 108–112,
    121, 135
        arson career of, 100,
            102–104, 110
        death of, 113
        visions of, 102–103, 111
sideshow attractions, 15–16
State Armory, *See*
    Connecticut State
    Armory

## T

teeth, *See* dental records
tent, *See* big top tent
Thompson, Dorothy Segee,
    101–102
Tuohy, Lynne, 86

## V

Versteeg, Edward
    "Whitey," 7, 88, **89**

## W

Wakefield, Patricia, 55,
    57
Wallenda, Carla, 21,
    42–44
Wallenda family 13, 18, 21,
    23, 27, 42–43, **44**
Walsh, Joseph, 20, 31
war bonds, 5
Weissenborn, Walter, 69–
    70, 72, 74, 128
Willet, Phyllis, **60**
World War II, 4, 47, 54, 83
    and circuses, 5
    disaster preparedness,
        47

## Y

Yee, James, 64, 72–73, 76

## Z

Zaccaro, Nicholas, **46**